D0342789

	DATE DUE		
NOV 23 '94			
FEB 01 '95			
MAY 10 '98			
DEC 03 '98			
FEB 05 '99			
MAY 26 '99			

PRISONS
A System in Trouble

Ann E. Weiss

ENSLOW PUBLISHERS, INC.

Bloy St. & Ramsey Ave.   P.O. Box 38
Box 777   Aldershot
Hillside, N. J. 07205   Hants GU12 6BP
U.S.A.   U.K.

Library of Congress Cataloging-in-Publication Data

Weiss, Ann E., 1943-
    Prisons : a system in trouble.

    Bibliography: p.
    Includes index.
    1. Summary: Discusses the current prison system and
such problems as arbitrary sentencing, overcrowding, and
the treatment of juvenile offenders.
    1. Prisons--United States--Juvenile literature.
2. Corrections--United States--Juvenile literature.
3. Juvenile corrections--United States--Juvenile
literature. [1. Prisons] I. Title.
 HV9471.W45   1988   365'.973   88-431
ISBN 0-89490-165-6

Printed in the United States of America

10 9 8 7 6 5 4 3 2

This book is dedicated to my aunt
Ruth H. Charlton
with many thanks

ACKNOWLEDGMENTS

The author wishes to thank the following for their invaluable assistance: Mary Ann Hawkes, Professor of Sociology and Criminal Justice, Rhode Island College; Milton G. Rector, President Emeritus, National Council on Crime and Delinquency; Roberta Richman, Director of Educational Services, Rhode Island Department of Corrections; Lieutenant Gerald R. Silva, Administrator, Lincoln County Jail, Wiscasset, Maine; and Priscilla Damon.

Contents

Foreword

Young people should enjoy this excellent book. It presents an honest and absorbing insight into the United States criminal justice system. An increasing number of young people are going to find employment and professional careers in some sector of that system where, at present, prisons are a core problem.

As voters and taxpayers, young people will find that the decisions made about our prisons and the purposes they serve will bear directly upon the kind of society we will have. Whether we can much longer afford the direction our criminal justice system is headed is a key question and should be considered by all concerned citizens.

Milton G. Rector
President Emeritus
National Council on Crime
and Delinquency

1

Riot!

The riot at South Carolina's Kirkland Correctional Institution broke out on Tuesday, April 1, 1986. It started at approximately 7:30 P.M. when one high-security inmate escaped from his cell. Wielding a homemade knife, the inmate seized a guard—Correctional Officer (C.O.)—and threatened to kill him. The C.O. tore loose and fled, dropping his keys as he ran to alert officers in the prison's centralized command post.

Suddenly, about half a dozen other similarly armed prisoners appeared on the scene. Accounts vary as to exactly what happened next, but somehow inmates managed to isolate seven C.O.s in one cell block and keep them trapped there. The inmates also used the first C.O.'s keys to release more than seven hundred of their fellow prisoners, who charged into the courtyard, where they milled around uneasily. A few fires were set—no one is sure by whom—and flames spurted from several buildings.

As prison riots go, the one at Kirkland was rather tame. The trapped C.O.s were quickly rescued by a platoon of officers carrying nightsticks and shields. The fires were

9

quenched, the released prisoners herded back into their cells, and the apparent instigators of the riot placed under heavily armed guard. Two prison employees reported slight cuts and bruises, and damage from the fires was later estimated at about $1.5 million. By midnight the uprising was over, and people were asking why it had ever begun.

Why had it? That question probably has almost as many possible answers as there were people involved in the disturbance itself. "Overcrowding" could be one. Kirkland, like virtually every other correctional facility in the country, operates at well over its original planned capacity. Designed to hold 448 prisoners, it had a total population of nearly a thousand on the night of the riot.

Such crowding has a profound impact on prisoners' lives. At the Maine State Prison in Thomaston, which is overcrowded but not so much so as Kirkland, a visiting reporter took note of that impact. "Some inmates," he informed his readers, "are forced to live doubled up in a six- by seven-foot cell." Six feet by seven feet means forty-two square feet of living space for two adults. According to guidelines issued by the American Correctional Association (ACA), an organization of about 20,000 U.S. and Canadian corrections professionals, a living space should amount to a minimum of sixty square feet for each prisoner.

Being cooped up in such a tiny cell entails more than just a loss of personal space, the reporter went on. A cell for two may contain a single bed, leaving one inmate to sleep on the floor. Since not merely the cells but the prison as a whole is overcrowded, thirty or forty men may have to share one toilet, shower, and sink. At some prisons, authorities have dealt with the overcrowding problem by converting classrooms, vocational-training centers, or infirmaries into dormitory quarters. The result is reduced educational and job-training opportunities and cuts in medical services.

10

Prison life is grim in other ways. Many of the nation's prisons were built in the nineteenth century, and efforts to modernize them have seldom, if ever, succeeded. Parts of the Thomaston facility, for example, date back to 1825, well before the days of central heating. Today prisoners housed on the building's ground level are routinely allotted three heavy woolen blankets, so cold are their cells during the long New England winter. Three levels above them, inmates swelter year-round in temperatures that rarely dip below 90° Fahrenheit. And prisoners here, like those in every other prison in the country, have plenty of additional complaints. "Lousy food," one called out to the reporter as he toured the plant. "No recreation on Saturdays and Sundays" and "No exercise" were other gripes.

But is it boredom, bad food, and overcrowding that lead to rioting and rebellion? No, says William Leeke, corrections commissioner for the state of South Carolina and a veteran of prison administration. Such conditions may have been a factor in the Kirkland trouble, he told news reporters, but at bottom, the riot was the work of "hard-core, violent-type inmates." As Leeke put it, "There's a small hard core of inmates who don't want anything to improve their lives." Clearly, in his view, improving conditions would do little to reduce prison violence.

Leeke is not the only penologist—expert in prison management—who thinks that way. "The worst feature of American prisons," wrote Jackson Toby, a sociology professor at New Jersey's Rutgers University, in 1986, "is the other prisoners." Toby, director of Rutgers' Institute for Criminological Research, cited as the number-one problem in the nation's prisons the brutality that the inmates display toward one another: the intimidation, beatings, and assaults, some of them sexual, that younger, weaker prisoners often suffer at the

11

hands of the older and stronger inmates. As for American prisons themselves, they are "almost luxurious," Professor Toby contends, especially compared to those in the under-developed countries of Asia, Africa, and Latin America. He lists the "amenities" to be found in U.S. prisons: beds and mattresses, flush toilets, "wholesome" food, heated cells and workshops, telephones, libraries, medical and dental care. To this list many prison critics would add radios and television sets. The fact that convicted criminals are permitted to watch hours and hours of TV every day is a special irritant to those who maintain that U.S. prison life is not tough enough.

One advocate of stricter prisons is a man named J. J. Maloney. "Many prisons offer more comfort than the U.S. Army offered its soldiers in 1959," he asserted in a 1983 article in *Saturday Review* magazine. Maloney would like to see that change. His prescription for prisons: "No jobs . . . no cigarettes, coffee, or candy bars . . . no personal radios or televisions. No phone calls. . . . Curtailed correspondence and one visit a month." Unlike Toby, who has studied prisons and prison life from the outside, Maloney has had firsthand experience with both. Convicted of murder as a teenager, he spent thirteen years in the Missouri State Penitentiary before being released in 1972. Today Maloney is a published poet and novelist as well as an award-winning journalist. If anyone can speak with authority about what prisons are—and ought to be—like, it is surely he.

Or is it? "Our criticism of Maloney is that he goes too far." So say two other ex-prisoners, John Irwin and Rick Mockler. Making prison life harsher, the two assert, will serve no good purpose. "Being locked away from one's family and friends, being totally out of control of one's life, is a deprivation that dwarfs the significance of television, stereos," and other amenities, they wrote in 1984. Their article first appeared in *The California Prisoner,* the monthly newsletter of the Prisoners' Union, a group of present and former inmates.

The goal of the Prisoners' Union is to change prison life by changing the relationship between prisoners and those who guard them. Even men and women convicted of a crime should retain certain legal and human rights, members believe. C.O.s should not be permitted to harass prisoners, for instance, or to treat them with unnecessary brutality. Prisoners should have a lawyer present when they face a prison disciplinary board, should receive a fair wage for any work they do while serving their sentences, and should be permitted to retain a measure of dignity and individuality. Only if prisoners are treated like responsible human beings will they be able to take on the responsibilities of living in "free-world" society after they are released, the Prisoners' Union maintains. "There is simply no evidence that making prisons harsher will make them more effective," Irwin and Mockler wrote.

Effectiveness—that's another issue. How effective are U.S. prisons today? Not very, most penologists admit. True, putting people in prison isolates them for a few months or years, and during that time, they are unable to commit new crimes against society. But what happens when their release dates come around? According to one study, about half of state prisoners are repeat offenders. The state of Michigan reported that 90 percent of those entering prison there in 1984 had already served time for serious crimes. This high rate of recidivism—falling back into criminal habits—may be one indication that prisons are not doing their job.

And that raises the final, and perhaps the most fundamental, question. What is a prison's job? What is it that we in the United States expect—or hope—our prison system will accomplish for us?

2

Of Punishments and Prisons

There's no question about why Wilbert Rideau went to prison back in 1961. Black and from a poverty-stricken background, Rideau was a nineteen-year-old junior high school dropout in those days. He had no job and no job skills. Limited to the most menial of part-time work, seemingly doomed to stay forever at the bottom of America's social and economic ladder, Rideau saw his life as meaningless and without direction.

One day he changed all that. Armed with a knife and a gun, Rideau walked into a bank in Lake Charles, Louisiana, grabbed three tellers as hostages, and forced them to accompany him to a quiet country road outside of town. There he shot and wounded all three. When one of them, a woman, sobbed and begged for her life, Rideau bent over and ruthlessly knifed her to death.

Arrested and charged with first-degree murder—deliberate, premeditated killing—Rideau was put on trial, convicted, and sentenced to die in Louisiana's electric chair. But there were delays in carrying out the sentence, and Rideau was still on death row in 1972. That was the year the United States

15

Supreme Court, the nation's highest court of law, overturned the death penalty in the states that then had capital punishment. Louisiana and thirty-five other states later rewrote their death-penalty laws in a way that the Court found acceptable. Even so, the 1972 ruling meant that Rideau's sentence (and that of everyone else then under similar sentence in the United States) was permanently commuted—set aside. Rideau settled down to life in Louisiana's maximum-security Angola Prison.

Unlike his earlier life, though, this was life with a purpose. By the 1970s, Rideau was reading, studying, educating himself, and working at becoming a writer. In 1976, he and a fellow inmate were named coeditors of Angola's convict-run newspaper, *The Angolite*. Under their direction, *The Angolite* collected honors: Columbia University's George Polk Award, the Robert F. Kennedy Award, and two Silver Gavel awards from the American Bar Association (ABA), an organization that represents the U.S. legal profession. In 1978, *The Angolite* was a finalist for a National Magazine Award.

Rideau in 1986 and Rideau twenty-five years earlier seemed to be two completely different personalities. "That person [I used to be] is a stranger to me now," Rideau told one reporter. "I don't even know him. I don't want to know him." Rideau had grown from what he called a "suicidal rebel" into a respected journalist. More important, prison life appeared to have brought Rideau to a clear understanding of the terrible nature of his crime and to have given him a firm determination to atone for it by leading a law-abiding and productive life in the future. He seemed to have been completely reformed—formed anew—by his prison experience.

He had also been punished by it. A quarter of a century in prison—a decade with the threat of execution hanging over his head—that's a longer, harsher sentence than many American murderers receive. Prison had served another purpose in Rideau's life as well. It had kept him off the streets and made it impossible for him to commit new crimes. Perhaps it had kept others from committing crimes, too. How many potential criminals may have been stopped—deterred—from robbing and murdering because they were afraid that what had happened to Rideau might happen to them? Deterrence, punishment, and reform—prison seemed to have accomplished them all in Rideau's case. Why then, some people were asking, was he still behind bars in 1986? We'll start to answer that question by taking a look at the history of prisons.

It is not a very long history. Prisons as we know them in the United States today, prisons like Angola, have been in existence for only about two hundred years. Before that, society had other ways of dealing with those found guilty of committing crimes. It is in those ways that the roots of our modern prisons lie.

In the oldest times, criminal justice was direct, simple, and harsh. "Life for life"—that was the ancient Hebrew tradition. "Eye for eye, tooth for tooth, hand for hand, foot for foot," the Old Testament dictates. Whatever violence one person committed against another, that same violence was to be done to him. "Burning for burning, wound for wound, stripe for stripe." Even animal behavior was made part of this primitive justice. An ox that gored a man or woman to death was to be stoned until it too died. Apparently, in Old Testament times, no one thought of simply restraining the beast and keeping it away from other people it might injure. No one thought of restraining human beings, either, or of punishing crimes of physical violence by depriving the criminal of his or her freedom.

Nor were people punished with imprisonment if they committed a crime against property. For thieves and robbers, res-

17

titution—making good the loss—was the prescribed remedy. In fact, the loss might have to be made more than good. The Old Testament penalty for stealing an ox was repayment in the amount of five oxen. A man who stole a sheep had to repay the animal's owner with four sheep. Once restitution had been made, the thief's punishment was over. He was free to go his way.

Other people of the long-ago Middle East had similar ideas about how justice should be administered. It was the Hebrews' neighbors and frequent enemies, the Babylonians, who gave the world its first known written criminal code. Drawn up nearly four thousand years ago during the reign of King Hammurabi, this code also prescribed direct physical retribution for crimes of violence and restitution for non-violent offenses. But strict as they were, both Hammurabi's Code and Old Testament law were based on a kind of fairness. Each reflected the idea that punishment should match the crime—not exceed it. A person could not be put to death for blinding someone, for example, or required to repay in oxen for a less-valuable sheep.

Even in the earliest societies, however, the punishment did not always fit the crime, and justice sometimes became more complex than "an eye for an eye." In Genesis, the first book of the Bible, we read how Adam and Eve's son Cain killed his brother Abel. But Cain was not forced to surrender his own life in return. Instead, God banished the murderer, sending him away to live the lonely life of a friendless wanderer. As a matter of fact, God took care to protect Cain from other would-be avengers. "And the Lord set a mark upon Cain, lest any finding him should kill him."

Banishment and exile have served as punishments in many times and places. Two thousand years ago, during the days of the Roman Empire, a woman caught in adultery might be

18

condemned to spend the rest of her life on a deserted rocky island, cut off from human society. Other forms of banishment were less formal. Murderers and thieves fleeing from justice might seek shelter in the vast tracts of wilderness that lay between the widely scattered towns and villages of the ancient world. Or they might be driven there by authorities eager to see the last of them. Hard pressed to survive on their own in the untamed forests, the banished commonly joined together in outlaw bands. Similar bands existed hundreds of years later in many parts of the world, providing inspiration for legends like those that grew up around the thirteenth-century English outlaw Robin Hood and his "merry men."

More recently, banishment has gone under the name of "deportation" or "transportation." England began deporting certain criminals—chiefly petty thieves and vagabonds—to its American colonies around the beginning of the seventeenth century. The colony of Georgia was settled in the mid-1700s by English deportees under the leadership of James Oglethorpe. By the end of the century, though, America was an independent nation, and the British had to find a new place to which they could transport their criminals. They chose Australia, another colonial possession. The French and the Russians also found it convenient to transport their offenders to far-off places. For France, one such spot was Devil's Island, part of that country's great prison colony in the Caribbean Sea. For Russians, exile meant remote, barren Siberia. During the time of the czars, who ruled Russia until the communist revolution of 1917, both criminal offenders and political prisoners were routinely banished to lonely settlements and labor camps there. After the revolution, Siberia remained a place of exile. No one knows precisely how many present-day Russian lawbreakers and political dissidents—men and women who have spoken against the Soviet system—may be hidden away in Siberia right now. Other modern countries that use some form of banishment to silence and control political opposition include South Africa and several of the dictatorships of Latin America.

Another means societies have found to deal with convicts is to enslave them. Loss of citizenship—reduction to slave status—was a common punishment in the ancient world. In some places, convict-slaves were set to working long, hard hours mining ores and quarrying marble for buildings and monuments. In others, they were placed aboard great galley ships and forced to pull the massive oars that sent those ships speeding across the sea. Chained to their benches, unwashed and ill fed, galley slaves were whipped and beaten into obedience and superhuman feats of strength. Forced labor was also the lot of English prisoners in Australia and of French convicts in the Caribbean. It is still the rule for many of the exiles of Siberia.

Capital punishment—the death penalty—and corporal punishment—the inflicting of bodily pain—are two other ways human beings have found to deal with transgressors. Both, of course, were part of the "life for a life, eye for an eye" codes of the very first civilizations. By Greek and Roman times, however, capital and corporal punishments were being handed out with little regard for the criminal's actual offense. Thieves as well as murderers might be put to death. Whipping was the penalty for a variety of crimes, not just for the crime of whipping someone else. A robber might have his hand cut off or be mutilated in some other fashion, but he would not necessarily be required to make restitution to his victim. Justice was no less harsh in the time of Christ than it had been under the most ancient of laws. But it had moved far away from the ancient standards of fairness.

At the end of the second century A.D., Rome fell under

increasing attack from the fierce tribes of northern and eastern Europe, and in 476 the Roman Empire finally collapsed. This collapse marked the start of the so-called Dark Ages of medieval Europe, a period that was to last for nearly a thousand years. During that time, European "justice" was a rough, cruel affair. Roman codes of law were largely forgotten, and it was a while before new formal, written rules took their place. Penalties were handed out arbitrarily, and death was the punishment for numerous offenses, including such "crimes" as sexual misconduct, witchcraft, and cowardice in battle. The list of capital crimes grew until, by the early 1800s, in England a person over the age of sixteen could be executed for any one of 222 offenses. Some of them—stealing a loaf of bread, for example—could send a ten-year-old to the gallows.

Offenders not put to death might be punished in other gruesome ways. Torture was commonplace in medieval Europe, and criminals were frequently compelled to endure it in public, much to the delight of the crowds that gathered to watch and jeer. Branding was another often-used form of corporal punishment. Every city had its share of unfortunates whose foreheads bore the indelible letter that signaled a particular crime—*T* for *thief, V* for *vagrant,* and the like—warning the world to shun and distrust them. Lesser criminals might be sentenced to sit in the stocks, heads and hands clamped into place through narrow openings between heavy boards. Anyone in the stocks was a natural target of abuse, both verbal and physical.

Another ingenious device of punishment was the ducking stool. Looking rather like a giant seesaw, the ducking stool rested on a fulcrum and had a small seat at one end. Strapped into the seat, the criminal could be lowered into a pond or river and held underwater for as long and as often as the authorities decreed. What sort of crime brought a person to the ducking stool? Gossiping and nagging were two. Still other criminal acts might be punished by the levying of a fine. Not only did a fine constitute punishment for the guilty; fines also served to enrich many a medieval king or nobleman.

Fines, ducking stools and the stocks, brandings and torture, death, enslavement or banishment—these were for centuries the chief punishments of western Europe. That is not to suggest that places of imprisonment did not exist as well. They did. But for the most part, medieval prisons were different from modern ones and were intended to serve a different function.

To begin with, imprisonment was generally reserved for political and religious offenders. The noble who had displeased his lord, the priest who criticized his superiors, the king's son who plotted to seize his father's throne—these were the people who ended up locked in a cell. The thief or murderer might be confined as well, but only for the short time it took until his real punishment—death, torture, or whatever—could be applied. Political prisoners knew they might be restrained for much longer periods.

How much longer, though, they could rarely guess. In medieval days, men and women were almost never imprisoned for specific, definite terms. Depending upon the ruler's mood and the political situation, a prisoner might be released—or executed—at any time. In 1173 King Henry II of England locked up his wife Eleanor after she and their sons led an unsuccessful revolt against him. Henry kept Eleanor prisoner for twelve long years before finally relenting and setting her free.

Medieval prisons also varied greatly in their physical comforts. Eleanor passed her time as a captive surrounded by all the trappings of royalty. Unluckier individuals, many of them noble, were confined in moldy dungeons where water trickled down cold, stony walls and rats scurried across the floor. Worst of all was to be thrown into an oubliette. An oubliette (from the French word *oublier,* "to forget") was a tiny cell deep underground, its only opening a small hole at the top. Leading straight upward from this hole was a long, narrow shaft. The prisoner was lowered into the oubliette, or dropped in, generally breaking some bones in the process. Food might occasionally be tossed in after him, or it might not. And there he would stay, truly forgotten by the powerful in the world above, until his moans faded away and he perished.

To the castle, the dungeon, and the oubliette was added, in 1166, a new type of place of confinement: the jail.

The first jails were established in England, by the same king who later imprisoned his own wife for treason. Jails were necessary, Henry II decided, because English men and women who found themselves accused of committing a crime did not always stay around long enough to face the charges. Instead, the accused had a habit of disappearing into the wilds to take up the outlaw life. What was required, Henry thought, was a system of lockups where people could be confined until they were brought to justice. Each county in the land was ordered to build a jail. The counties were not, however, required to pay for supporting jail populations. The confined had to buy their own food, firewood, and other necessities. They also often found it desirable to bribe the guards to allow them special privileges, such as the right to have visitors or to exercise out-of-doors. Bribes saved prisoners from beatings and other physical punishments, as well. All in all, in these early English jails, it was better to be rich than poor.

Jails represented an important step on the road to our modern prison system. Another step was the workhouse, an institution that emerged in the sixteenth century, as medieval habits and customs began giving way to a more modern and humane outlook.

Among the first of Europe's workhouses was one that opened in London in 1557 in an abandoned palace. Officially called the London House of Correction, the institution became known as Bridewell because of its location near St. Bride's Well. Its purpose was to provide a living place for homeless boys who might otherwise have caused trouble or turned to lives of crime, but it was not long before London authorities recognized Bridewell as an ideal dumping ground for the unwanted of their society: runaways, orphans, prostitutes, criminals, and the mentally handicapped and insane. Good intentions bowed to poor practices, and four hundred years later the word *bridewell* still signifies a place of squalor and degradation.

In a few workhouses, such as the Hospice of San Michele in Rome, conditions were better. San Michele was set up in 1704 by Clement XI, pope of the Roman Catholic Church. It was an institution for wayward boys, but not one to which the boys were sent for punishment. Rather, they were taught to work, to pray, and to meditate. Repentance and the formation of good habits—these were the goals at San Michele. Penitence, not punishment, was also the goal at a workhouse established in Ghent, Belgium, in 1771. The Ghent workhouse was the inspiration of a reformer named Jean Jacques Vilain.

Among Vilain's most enthusiastic admirers was an Englishman, John Howard. Howard's goal was to adapt Vilain's workhouse reforms to the prison. In 1777, he published a book entitled *The State of the Prisons in England and Wales,* in which he deplored the nation's bridewells and called for the founding of new prisons along the lines pioneered by Vilain and Pope Clement. Sanitary surroundings, humane conditions, and, above all, a regimen that encouraged penitence on the part of the inmates—these were Howard's ideals. Two years later, he, along with a number of English Quakers—members of the Society of Friends—persuaded the British Parliament to pass the Penitentiary Act of 1779. Although the birth of the penitentiary system did not spell an immediate end to the cruel treatment of English convicts, it did herald the beginning of a new age in penology.

The State of the Prisons made its mark in the United States as well. Up to the time of the American Revolution, justice in most of the colonies reflected justice in England. Execution was a common punishment. Even children could be put to death for stealing or for disobeying their parents. Whippings, brandings, the stocks, and the ducking stool were as familiar in America as in Europe. Banishment was as familiar, too. The colonies of Rhode Island and Connecticut were both established by men and women exiled from Massachusetts for their religious convictions.

After the Revolution, however, in America as in England, attitudes began to change. People who had been banished and otherwise punished began to rise to leadership positions. In 1791, the new United States adopted the first ten amendments to its federal Constitution. Eighth in this "Bill of Rights" was a prohibition against "cruel and unusual" punishments.

The Eighth Amendment did not forbid such penalties as whipping and capital punishment. Neither was considered cruel or unusual in the eighteenth century, and even today as many as 80 percent of the American people support death-penalty laws. This, incidentally, makes the United States unique among the world's industrialized democracies—it is the only one that still permits execution of criminals. In our fondness for this form of punishment, we Americans resemble the people of the Soviet Union, South Africa, and the Iran of

25

the Ayatollah Khomeini. A person in the United States can be put to death for a crime committed when he or she was as young as ten years old, and, in fact, nine states set *no* minimum age for executions.

But although the Eighth Amendment did nothing to prevent capital or corporal punishment, it did ensure that Americans would not be subjected to the harshest and most bizarre of Old World penalties and tortures. Before long, it was also clear that the United States was ready to experiment with the modern penitentiary system.

It was the Quakers of Philadelphia who led the movement to substitute prison terms for the older forms of punishment. In 1790, the Pennsylvania legislature voted to renovate the city's Walnut Street Jail to create a model penitentiary. One of the features of the new prison was that criminals were sent there to serve sentences of a fixed length of time. Another was that inmates were not required to pay for their own upkeep. The state took over that responsibility. A third reform concerned the classification of prisoners. Hardened criminals were separated from lesser offenders and housed apart from them. The latter lived together in large dormitories, but each of the former was put into a separate cell and confined there in solitude.

Solitude—that was the byword at the Walnut Street Jail. The Quakers believed firmly in the redemptive value of solitary living and meditation. Even the most wicked, they were sure, could be brought to a sense of wrongdoing and penitence through months or years of lonely contemplation. The Quakers believed in hard work, too, and every inmate of the new prison was assigned to labor at a useful craft—shoemaking, weaving, tailoring, and so on. But it was solitude, not work, that lay at the heart of the state's prison philosophy. When Pennsylvania opened its large Eastern State Penitentiary in 1829, it was run along strictly solitary lines. Impressed by the system's apparent humanity, other states began trying it out for themselves.

"This trial," two French visitors to the United States wrote in the 1830s, was "fatal to . . . the health of the criminals." Their words were true—in some cases, literally true. During the first year that New York's Auburn State Prison operated under the solitary system, authorities recorded the deaths of five inmates. The French observers summed up the reason for the fatalities: "Absolute solitude . . . is beyond the strength of man." They were right. What the high-minded Quaker reformers had not taken into account is that human beings are social animals with a powerful instinct to seek companionship and to live and work in groups. When that instinct is thwarted, stress builds, and physical and emotional illness often follows. That was what happened at Auburn. In addition to the five who died there, one went insane, and twenty-six others became so severely disturbed that they had to be pardoned and released. After that, Auburn switched to a different system, this one based upon silence.

The silent system turned out to be nearly as devastating for the confined as the solitary one. Besides being driven to socialize, people also need to communicate among themselves, to talk and to discuss, to share joy, anger, and sorrow. At Auburn, talking was not permitted. Inmates worked and ate in groups, but invariably they did so in total silence. Even nonverbal communication was forbidden. A movement of the lips or a turning of the head could merit a vicious beating from the guards.

From the 1830s on, the two systems, silent and solitary—Auburn and Pennsylvania—fought for supremacy in American penology. Yet almost from the start, it was clear that neither worked. Both were destructive to the prisoners' personalities, and neither one produced penitence or prevented recidivism. Fixed sentences were a hallmark of both systems, and fixed sentences had a drawback that the eighteenth-century reformers had also failed to anticipate. By making it impossible for prisoners to win early release through good behavior and hard work, such sentences destroyed much of their motivation to cooperate and try to mend their ways. Work programs quickly degenerated. Either no work was available, or prisoners were forced to labor at pointless and back-breaking jobs, such as smashing rocks. By the late 1860s, U.S. penologists—leaders of an emerging profession—were demanding new improvements in the nation's prisons. In 1870, a group of them met in Cincinnati, Ohio, to debate what form those improvements should take. Under the name of the Prison Congress (later the National Prison Association, then the American Prison Association, and today the American Correctional Association), the group plotted a new course for American prisons.

"Let us leave, for the present, the thought of inflicting punishment upon prisoners," Zebulon Brockway, warden of the Detroit House of Correction, pleaded to the assembled delegates. Instead of seeking revenge against convicted criminals—for what could inspire brutally enforced silence and life-threatening solitude but a desire for vengeance?—Brockway suggested prison should aim at "the protection of society by the prevention of crime, and reformation of criminals."

Soon thereafter, *reformation* replaced *penitence* as the key word in American penology. Six years after the Cincinnati meeting, Brockway was given the opportunity to try out his ideas at a new kind of prison in New York State.

The Elmira State Reformatory opened in 1876 as an institution for boys and young men. Perhaps already dubious about the likelihood of reforming older criminals, the New

28

York legislature decided that offenders over the age of thirty would continue to go to "the pen." But Brockway himself displayed confidence in the workability of his program. He established courses of education at Elmira, organized athletic events, and tried to see to it that inmates had opportunities for job training, military drill, and religious instruction—opportunities that were virtually nonexistent in the country's older prisons.

In another break with penitentiary practices, the reformatory did away with fixed sentences. Prisoners were to be held at Elmira only until the institution had done its job, that is, until they reformed. When by their attitudes and behavior they demonstrated that they had forsaken criminal ways, they would be paroled—released. Indeterminate sentencing and parole were regarded as forward-looking ideas in the 1870s, as were reformatories themselves. Institutions modeled upon Elmira began springing up all over the United States.

Unfortunately, they had little more success at preventing crime and ending criminal behavior than penitentiaries had. One reason for this was financial. The money needed to set up effective classes and programs was rarely forthcoming from state legislatures. Another reason for the reformatories' lack of success had to do with politics. Wardens and parole board members tended to be appointed to their positions on the basis of their friendships and political connections, rather than on the basis of their professional dedication and abilities.

A third problem turned out to be indeterminate sentencing. Prisoners quickly found that if they could learn to beat the system they stood a better chance of winning parole. Beating the system was not difficult: say the kind of words wardens and parole boards wanted to hear, act like the kind of person they wanted to see, hide anger and resentment behind a facade of genuine reform—this, inmates discovered, was the surest path to early freedom. No wonder so many of them were soon back in custody. Another problem with indeterminate sentencing was that prison authorities also learned to twist it to their advantage. The authorities did not hesitate to deny parole, even to those who deserved it, if they thought doing so would serve their own purposes. The denial could be a punishment for a minor infraction of prison rules, a warning to other prisoners, or simple vindictiveness.

But the biggest cause of the reformatories' failure to live up to expectations was a matter of attitude. Despite the enthusiasm reformers felt for indeterminate sentencing and for prison education and job-training programs, despite Brockway's stirring call for an end to vengeance in criminal justice, the people inside each prison—inmates and guards alike—never stopped seeing prison as a place of retribution. Just as ideals about meditation and penitence had earlier been transformed into the thinly disguised cruelties of the solitary and silent systems, so plans for putting aside punishment and concentrating instead on reforming and training soon came up against the old realities of prison life.

This is not to say that the reforms of the late nineteenth century failed utterly. On the contrary, they led to lasting improvements in prison conditions and laid a foundation for later, twentieth-century reform efforts. But the reforms of Brockway and others did fall short of achieving their goals. Prisons were still violent, dangerous places. Tensions remained high between the guards and the guarded. Anger remained as well, as did fear and brutality. And recidivism was as much a problem as ever.

The history of U.S. prisons after the turn of the century continued to be one of conflict between the ideal of what prison should be and the reality of what it is. The early part of the century saw a new wave of reform, this one aimed at a more scrupulous classification of criminals. Such classification, penologists suggested, would allow them to deal with prisoners on an individual basis, designing programs intended to help each to overcome the problems that had brought him or her to prison in the first place. More careful and detailed classification continues to be a prison reform goal today.

By the middle of the twentieth century, *rehabilitation* and *treatment* had become the watchwords. The idea behind the treatment philosophy was that many criminals are not so much wicked as they are disturbed or in need of learning new ways to behave. In 1955, a model "total treatment facility" for the criminally disturbed opened in Jessup, Maryland. Here, at the Patuxent Institution, the most advanced scientific methods, medicines, and psychiatric diagnoses and treatment were to be devoted to transforming wrongdoers into solid citizens. Prisoners could be released only when the psychiatrists agreed that they were "ready"—that they had been reformed.

Once again, fine-sounding theories battled ancient attitudes—and generally ended up losing. Psychiatrists, psychologists, and social workers set out to modify, or change, criminal behavior through what they termed therapy and negative reinforcement. Their patients (at Patuxent, prisoners were known as patients), however, saw little distinction between behavior modification and punishment. Much of the "therapy" at Patuxent was identical with the punishments of other prisons—hosings with powerful streams of water, beatings, and sprayings with chemical Mace. Additional "therapies" included painful electric shock treatments and the administration of tranquilizers and other drugs with potent and often unpleasant side effects. What Patuxent doctors labeled "negative reinforcement" their "patients" experienced as being locked up in solitary confinement, often for months on end. Less than twenty years after Patuxent opened its doors, a Maryland court ruled that conditions there violated the Eighth Amendment's prohibition against cruel and unusual punishment. Few wished to fight the ruling; by the 1970s, the enthusiasm for behavior modification was already dying out.

Behavior modification may no longer be a technique of prison management, but what is to take its place? What should prison be like for those who are confined there? Should a term behind bars change a person? How? What is it that we Americans want our prisons to accomplish? These are the questions with which we started this chapter, and they bring us right back to Wilbert Rideau and the reason he was still incarcerated in 1986.

Was Rideau being kept at Angola to bring him to penitence, as the Quakers of two hundred years ago would have had it? No. Rideau had long since expressed repentance for his crime.

Was he there to prevent him from committing new crimes? Perhaps. But how likely was it that an articulate and self-confident middle-aged professional would repeat the senseless crime of a desperate, suicidal teenager? Or was Rideau being held as a deterrent to other would-be criminals? If so, how effective a deterrent could he be? Are today's despairing youths going to think through what happened to Rideau and use his experience as a guide to their own actions? How many of them have even heard of Rideau?

Was Rideau in prison to be reformed or rehabilitated? How could he be? By 1986, he had given every indication that he was fully prepared to take his place as a decent member of society.

Why, then, was Rideau behind bars? To many Americans, only one answer seemed possible. He was at Angola because he had not yet satisfied society's desire for revenge. Rideau had taken a woman's life, and now that woman's fellow citizens would take his. They would not take it literally—the Supreme Court's 1972 death-penalty decision had made that impossible. But Rideau's chance to enjoy a normal life; to have a home, a family, a job; to be self-supporting; to contribute his best to the world; to be fully human—of that he was to be deprived. For underlying the idealism, the ringing words, the calls to reform, is society's demand for revenge against the guilty for the acts they have committed. Penitence, deterrence, reformation, rehabilitation, and treatment—each plays or has played a part in U.S. corrections. But it is vengeance to which we have given the leading role.

3

Prison Systems

Government in the United States operates on four separate
and distinct levels: national, state, county, and local. America's systems of criminal correction reflect the same four divisions.

On the national level, there is the federal prison system.
This system is made up of more than forty institutions built
largely to house men and women suspected or found guilty of
breaking federal laws. The federal system did not come into
being until 1891, a full century after the nation's first state
prison system—the one inaugurated by the 1790 rebuilding of
Philadelphia's Walnut Street Jail—was established. During
that century, federal authorities had no choice but to send
anyone convicted of violating a federal statute to one of the
country's state prisons. Now, at last, the U.S. Congress was
ready to correct that situation.

What Congress did in 1891 was to pass legislation setting
up three federal penitentiaries. The three—at Leavenworth,
Kansas; on McNeil's Island off the Washington coast; and in
Atlanta, Georgia—remain a part of the system to this day.

All were intended to house felons, those offenders whose crimes—felonies—include murder, rape, kidnapping, big-time robbery of federally protected entities, and treason. Because felons have committed what our society considers the most serious of crimes, they are generally regarded as the most violent and dangerous of criminals. Therefore, the prisons intended to hold them are designed to provide the maximum degree of security against escapes or riots and other disorders.

At maximum-security prisons, grounds and buildings are surrounded by high, fortresslike walls aimed at cutting the institution and its inmates off from the community outside. The walls are surmounted by towers and gun turrets. Armed C.O.s patrol the walls' top perimeters, keeping an eye out for trouble below.

Guns are seldom taken into the actual prison, however; the no-guns-where-prisoners-might-get-their-hands-on-them rule is one of the strictest in prison life. Electronic devices sensitive enough to detect the least hint of unauthorized movement are planted along possible escape routes, and by night, powerful searchlights can shed their glare into the remotest of corners. For the inmates themselves, regimentation, strict rules, and tough discipline are constants.

The penitentiaries constructed at Leavenworth, McNeil's Island, and Atlanta in the 1890s were only the start for the federal prison system. Early in the twentieth century, the growth in the number of female federal prisoners moved Congress to appropriate funds to build a facility to house them. The Federal Reformatory for Women opened in 1925 in West Virginia.

The 1920s also saw a rapid increase in the male federal prison population, an increase due largely to two factors: Prohibition and the automobile. Autos were rare when the twentieth century began, but by the twenties they were an everyday phenomenon. Auto theft had become an everyday affair as well, and Congress reacted to that fact by making it a federal crime to transport a stolen car across state lines. Prohibition, which put an end to the legal manufacture, sale, or transportation of alcoholic beverages in the United States, was provided for by the Eighteenth Amendment to the Constitution. The Prohibition amendment took effect in 1920. It was repealed thirteen years later by the Twenty-first Amendment, but not before it had inspired bootleggers—liquor smugglers—to commit thousands upon thousands of federal offenses.

The crime wave of the Prohibition era led not only to more new prisoners but also to the creation of one new federal law-enforcement agency and the reorganization of another. The reorganized agency was the Federal Bureau of Investigation (FBI), set up originally in 1908 as the Bureau of Investigation of the U.S. Justice Department. Today the FBI has the power to investigate possible crimes in nearly two hundred areas—espionage, kidnapping, bank robbery, interstate transportation of stolen property, and fraud against the government among them. The new agency, which Congress established in 1930, was the Bureau of Prisons. The Bureau of Prisons, too, is part of the Justice Department. Its job is overseeing and managing the entire federal prison system.

Today, the Bureau of Prisons is responsible for forty-five prison facilities nationwide. Six of them are penitentiaries, and another three are reformatories for adults. In addition, the bureau operates youth and juvenile institutions for offenders under the age of eighteen in Kentucky, Colorado, and West Virginia; prison camps in Florida, Alabama, and Arizona; a prison medical center in Missouri; and correctional

37

institutions in several other states. Federal Detention Centers in New York and Arizona house those awaiting trial on federal charges. Separate centers have been established to detain persons suspected of entering the country illegally.

Not all the institutions in the federal prison system are designed to provide maximum security. Many are medium- or minimum-security establishments. As their name suggests, medium-security prisons may appear less formidable than maximum-security ones. Thick walls and grim battlements may be replaced by chain-link fences topped with coils of sharply barbed wire. Prisoners who have demonstrated good behavior are allowed a certain freedom of movement, strolling unaccompanied along prison corridors or even walking outdoors from one building to another.

Minimum-security prisons offer still more freedom. Inmates are not subject to constant surveillance, and some of them may, within strict limits, leave the secure parts of the facility in order to work or study in communities outside. Minimum-security prisons offer other amenities—open, campuslike surroundings, attractive lounges, and accommodations that in some cases look more like tiny rooms than prison cells. Some of these prisons even boast of outdoor recreation facilities such as golf courses, swimming pools, or tennis courts. Among the men and women to be to be found in medium- and minimum-security institutions are felons who are considered nonviolent, or those who have already served part of their sentences under high security and who have been "promoted." Other lower-security inmates have been found guilty of lesser offenses such as assault, small theft, and the like, or of "white-collar crimes" like forgery and income tax evasion. Penalties for such offenses rarely amount to more than a year behind bars.

Least restrictive of all the institutions in the federal system are its prerelease centers. The first three prerelease centers, located in Los Angeles, Chicago, and New York, were set up by the Bureau of Prisons in 1961 as halfway houses to hold convicts nearly due for freedom. Since then, five more such centers have been added to the federal system. Prerelease prisoners may hold jobs in the community, visit frequently with friends and family, and receive special counseling in preparation for life on the outside.

In June 1986, the total federal prison population stood at 44,330, an all-time high. That year, the cost to taxpayers to maintain the federal prison system was over $530 million. To supervise this prison population, the Bureau of Prisons employed a force of over 10,500 C.O.s, administrators, and others. At the head of each prison in the federal system is a warden or superintendent. The warden is responsible for maintaining overall prison discipline. That means keeping minor disturbances from escalating into violence and rioting, preventing escapes, and making sure prisoners are not brutalized by other inmates or by those assigned to guard them.

Correctional Officers amount to between one-third and one-half of all bureau employees. The four thousand or so C.O.s in the federal system enforce discipline on a day-to-day basis. It is the C.O.s in any prison system who have the most contact with the prisoners, who tell prisoners what to do and when, where, and how to do it. They are authorized to report prisoners for violations of the rules and to bring them before a prison's disciplinary board for possible punishment. The qualifications needed to become a federal prison C.O. are not tough—a high school diploma and good health. Other staffers at federal prisons include social workers, teachers, vocational instructors, psychologists, doctors, nurses, and so on. Finally, there are the bureau administrators who work out of its Washington, D.C., headquarters.

The federal prison system is a complex one, composed as it is of various security levels, men's and women's prisons, institutions for adults and institutions for juveniles, and so forth. Yet compared to prisons on the next level of government, the state level, the federal system is relatively simple. That is because it is one single system, administered from the top by a single agency. State prison systems have all the diversity of the federal system—different levels of security; men's, women's, and youth divisions; penitentiaries, reformatories, correctional centers, facilities for the criminally insane, and halfway houses. But what makes state prisons so complicated to discuss is their number. Each state runs its own system, and so, for a grand total of fifty-one, does the commonwealth of Puerto Rico. Each system, like each state or jurisdiction, differs slightly from all the others.

We've already seen clues to the origins of some of the differences. Back in 1790, influenced by the ideas of men like John Howard, the Quakers of Philadelphia persuaded their state legislators to adopt the system of solitary confinement and meditation that was supposed to lead criminals to penitence. The state of New York copied the Pennsylvania model but, after its disastrous experiment at Auburn, modified it to create the silent system. As other states developed prison systems, they tended to follow New York's example. However, the silent system proved no more successful than the solitary one in producing repentance, and that meant the states had no great incentive to follow it in every detail. Gradually, over the years, each state changed and adapted its system to suit its own needs and the demands of its citizens.

Those needs and demands varied from state to state. States with expanding urban populations, for instance, experienced crime problems that more rural states did not. Then, as now, cities acted as magnets to attract orphans and runaways, and by the 1820s, numbers of homeless boys and girls were roaming the streets of the big cities of the Northeast. Many of the older ones turned to crime to support themselves, and the younger ones seemed likely to do the same. In 1825, New York became the first American city to open a House of Refuge for delinquent and "predelinquent" juveniles. Boston and Philadelphia quickly took similar actions. The nation's first reform school was founded in Massachusetts in 1846.

The same French visitors to the United States who, as we saw in Chapter 2, so vigorously condemned conditions at Auburn State Prison were enthusiastic about the Houses of Refuge. "The young delinquents are received much less for punishment than to receive that education which their parents or their ill-fate refused them," they wrote. Not only were the youngsters educated at the new institutions; they were carefully classified and separated according to the type and seriousness of their offenses and were promoted into "higher" classifications as their behavior improved. They were also allowed to take part in writing the rules by which they lived.

Authorities at the early Houses of Refuge were innovative in other ways. They introduced a form of indeterminate sentencing decades before Zebulon Brockway put the parole system into effect at the Elmira Reformatory. They offered follow-up supervision for juveniles after their release, assigning officers to keep track of those who had been freed and to monitor their progress. Any who committed new crimes were promptly reincarcerated. Although the Houses of Refuge were city institutions to begin with, they provided the basis for later statewide juvenile institution systems.

The fact that the first cities to tackle the problem of juvenile delinquency were in northern states is no coincidence. Throughout the eighteenth and nineteenth centuries, it was the North that led the way in U.S. prison development. The

Houses of Refuge, the idea that criminals could be brought to penitence, and the substitution of imprisonment for capital and corporal punishment—each of these developments showed up first in a northern institution. As southern officials planned their own prison systems, they sometimes imitated a northern idea, but seldom did they introduce new policies of their own. Right up to the time of the Civil War, which began between the Union states of the North and the Confederate states of the South in 1861, southern prisons lagged behind the more progressive institutions of the North.

Later on, the regional differences became even more pronounced. When the war ended with the surrender of the Confederacy in 1865, the South was in terrible shape. Its land was devastated by the fighting, its economy a shambles, its people demoralized. To make matters worse, the victorious North imposed strict military rule upon the South, a rule that lasted in some states until 1870. Struggling to recover from the war, Southerners had little time, money, or energy to devote to their prisons. Even as Indiana's Zebulon Brockway was calling for prison reform in Ohio and putting his ideas into operation in New York, guards and wardens in states to the south were reverting to the traditions of a crueler past.

One reversion was bringing back the custom of requiring prisoners to pay for their own upkeep. No longer would the states of the South support their prison populations. Instead, southern prisoners were to earn their way by being thrown into a condition closely resembling slavery.

For some convicts, semislavery took the form of assignment to a chain gang. Clapped into leg irons and linked together with heavy chains, the men on a gang repaid the state for their board and room by building public roads or chopping brush along them. Twelve-hour working days were not uncommon for members of a chain gang, and discipline was by whip and gun. For other prisoners, paying their way meant being hired out to private individuals as "contract labor." Under the contract, the owner of a business or industry promised to assume responsibility for feeding, clothing, housing, and disciplining the prisoners. In return, the state tacitly agreed to "look the other way" while the contractors saved money by half-starving their prisoners and upped their profits by brutally driving them to harder and harder work. Contract labor was outlawed earlier in this century, and men no longer work chained together under a southern sun, but among prisoners, prisons in the South have traditionally had a more sinister reputation than those of the North.

In all, almost 485,000 men and women were incarcerated in the country's 626 state correctional institutions in mid-1986. As with the federal prison population, this figure represented a record high. The staff setup in state prisons reflects that of federal institutions. A warden heads each institution, C.O.s—who do not necessarily have a full high school education—oversee the prisoners' daily activities, and instructors, social workers, doctors, and others provide special services. Altogether, 172,138 men and women were employed in early 1985 by state prison systems.

When it comes to county and local corrections, systems are even more varied than they are on the state level. That is hardly surprising: the United States has fifty states and more than sixty times as many counties—a total of 3,047 separate systems. Add to this the nation's city systems, perhaps as many as two thousand in all. Then count in its tens of thousands of police precinct lockups in which suspects may be held for a few hours or days before being sent to jail, and you have an overwhelming number of institutions. Most are administered separately, although some cities and counties—Washington, D.C., New York City, and Cook County, Illinois, among them—have established corrections departments of their own. With a few exceptions, these local and county institutions are jails, rather than prisons.

There is a difference. Prisons are for those men and women who have been pronounced guilty of a crime. Jails, instituted in twelfth-century England as holding places for those awaiting trial, still have that as their main function today, although offenders who have committed misdemeanors serve their sentences in a jail rather than in a prison. As we saw earlier in this chapter, the federal system also includes jails. At that level they are known as detention centers. On the state level, jails have a variety of names; one state's Awaiting Trial Unit is another state's Intake Service Center.

Not everyone who is accused of a crime is detained in jail prior to trial. In some cases, detainees are allowed to participate in pretrial release programs that allow them to remain free but under some form of supervision. In other cases, the accused person is allowed to go free after posting bail. Posting bail means putting up a sum of money—a greater or smaller amount depending upon the seriousness of the charge—as a guarantee that he or she will show up for trial. If the person does show up, the money is returned. But if he or she disappears—"jumps bail"—the money is sacrificed.

In general, people end up spending time in jail for one of two reasons. The first is poverty. People who cannot afford bail are confined until their trial dates come up. Sometimes a needy defendant can get around that problem by borrowing the required sum from a bail bondsman. Such a bondsman is in the business of lending bail money and collecting interest on it. Unless the bondsman is sure that the accused can repay the loan, though, or is positive that he or she will appear in court, the loan will not be forthcoming.

Another reason for a suspect's having to stay in jail could

be that the crime of which he or she stands accused is extremely serious. If prosecutors—the lawyers who bring cases against the accused on behalf of the government—can convince a judge that a defendant is too dangerous to be at large, or likely to leave town despite having posted bond, he or she will be denied bail. In 1987, the U.S. Supreme Court upheld a federal law that permits judges to order a denial of bail and "preventive detention" for defendants who might endanger "the safety of any other person and the community." Rapists, child molesters, and the like are among those for whom preventive detention is a possibility. Civil liberties groups around the country objected strongly to the Court's ruling, arguing that imposing preventive detention, like refusing bail in other cases, may result in a defendant's having to spend a year or more in jail before his or her trial can be scheduled. This practice smacks of the kind of criminal "justice" found in such undemocratic countries as South Africa and the Soviet Union, civil libertarians claimed. It turns the U.S. tradition of "innocent until proven guilty" into "guilty unless you can prove yourself innocent."

Because of the sheer number of jails and lockups around the country, and because most are separately administered, it is even harder to generalize about them than it is about state correctional facilities. Jails vary enormously from county to county and city to city. The Lincoln County Jail, in the coastal resort town of Wiscasset, Maine, for example, is housed in the lower level of the Sheriff's Department building. The building opened in 1985. Its brick exterior blends harmoniously with the town's graceful Federal-style architecture. Inside, the jail's dozen or so cells and seven-bed dormitory hold a maximum of twenty prisoners and detainees. Inmates are strictly segregated according to age and sex. Juveniles are never allowed to so much as catch sight of an adult offender.

The cells are bare but scrupulously clean. A heavily fenced courtyard affords space for each inmate to exercise daily; a small library doubles as a visiting room, and cable television is provided, although prisoners are not allowed private sets. The jail is quiet, the C.O.s are firm but pleasant, and the supervisor knows every inmate by name and speaks compassionately of each one.

At the other end of the spectrum are jails like New York City's Riker's Island facility. Started in the 1930s, with a present capacity of 12,858, the six separate buildings on Riker's Island held 14,150 men, women, and juveniles in October 1986. There city and state parole violators, pretrial detainees and runaways battle sentenced drug addicts, sex offenders, and murderers for precious living space in overcrowded cells and dorms. "This place is a zoo," one frightened seventeen-year-old told a reporter. So overcrowded is Riker's Island that New York has started using old ferry boats to house some of its inmates.

Because jails cover so many jurisdictions, figures about overall populations at any given time are hard to come by. Is a man who is held in a New York City police precinct station for forty-eight hours before being moved to Riker's Island counted as a lockup statistic or as a jail statistic? What if he is released on bail after two weeks at Riker's Island? Because of confusion or delays in reporting the statistics, he may be included in both counts—or in neither. Monetary figures are just as tricky to assess. City and county budgets are complex documents, and it is not always clear exactly how much of any particular sum is going into jails, how much into routine law enforcement, how much into court costs, and the like.

Still other factors confuse the U.S. corrections picture. The four systems—federal, state, county, and local—are not entirely separate. In some instances, federal prisoners may be sent to serve their sentences in state or county facilities. This could be done to allow the prisoner to continue to work at his or her job, or because a particular jail or prison has a unique program from which a judge believes the prisoner can benefit. When a federal prisoner does go to a nonfederal facility, the federal government pays board. By the same token, jail inmates may find themselves in state or federal institutions, their board paid by the government that has jurisdiction over them, from time to time. In 1986, four outbreaks of serious violence in one week at Riker's Island led officials there to move seventy-two ringleaders to state prisons elsewhere. One state may even arrange a transfer of certain inmates to facilities in other states. Just before Christmas 1986, fifty-nine of Alaska's "most dangerous" convicts were flown to Minnesota prisons and held there to await the scheduled 1987 opening of Alaska's first maximum-security institution. Interstate Compacts have been authorized by federal and state statutes to permit such transfers.

Sometimes jails, prisons and other facilities may seem to be all mixed up together. Minimum-, medium-, and maximum-security cells and dormitories, an Awaiting Trial Unit, and housing for the criminally insane may be located on a single campus or even in a single building. A prerelease center may stand just across the street.

Furthermore, complex as the U.S. system of jails and prisons is, and despite its record number of inmates, that system and those inmates represent only the tip of the iceberg as far as overall corrections are concerned. Parolees—men, women, and juveniles—are also considered part of corrections. So are those allowed out of jail on bail. So are those on probation. Probation, pioneered first in Massachusetts, then in Vermont and Rhode Island at the very end of the nineteenth century, is similar to parole in that it allows a convicted person to live under supervision in the outside world rather than in prison. The difference between the two is that while parole is granted to someone who has already served part of his or her sentence, probation substitutes for a prison or jail sentence. The individual sentenced to probation must visit a probation officer regularly and comply with court-ordered conditions to demonstrate that he or she is living a law-abiding life. Failure to report on schedule, to comply with probation conditions, or participation in any new criminal activity, may result in an end to probation and a start to serving time.

People on probation and parole, people free on bail, people in jail, and people in prison all help to make up the hundreds of thousands of those within the correctional systems of the United States today. How many in all? A full 1.5 percent of the entire adult population of the country, the federal government estimated in 1986. That's a small percentage, but a lot of people—somewhere around two and a half million of them. Yet, according to some experts in the field, thousands of other lawbreakers never become part of the system at all.

4

Getting Into Prison

Want to go to prison? Getting there may not be as easy as you think—even if you commit a crime first.

That may sound odd, but the statistics bear the statement out. In 1980, one hundred thirty thousand men and women were arrested on felony charges in New York State. Just eight thousand of them, approximately one-sixteenth, were found guilty and sentenced to prison within that year.

Nationwide, the statistics are even more startling. Writing in 1984, newspaper columnist Allan C. Brownfeld quoted figures showing that "for every five hundred serious crimes, just twenty adults and five juveniles . . . are sent to jail—a ratio of one in twenty." In fact, the ratio is more like one out of a hundred, or so a group called the Prison Research Education Action Project (PREAP) claims. According to PREAP, only half of all crimes ever get into the statistics to begin with. "In one study," PREAP says, "out of a hundred major crimes [felonies]: fifty were reported to the police; suspects were arrested in twelve of the cases; six persons were convicted; one or two went to prison."

Such figures sound appalling, but do they really tell the whole story? Isn't it possible, for instance, that each of the "one or two" who does go to prison was actually responsible for several, perhaps many, of the hundred original crimes? It is also important to remember that the numbers may not be totally accurate. Consistent and reliable crime and prison statistics are hard to come by. Still, the numbers cannot be dismissed out of hand, and it is undeniable that many in this country do commit crimes and remain free. Nevertheless, there are factors that can dramatically increase a person's chances of landing in prison. Among them:

• *Being male.* Over 95 percent of all U.S. prisoners are men and boys. According to *The Corrections Yearbook* for 1985, published by the Criminal Justice Institute, Inc., of South Salem, New York, one state, New Hampshire, reported no adult female prisoners at all that year.

• *Being young.* Most prisoners in the United States fall between the ages of 15 and 30. In 1985, the average age was 28.2 years. (This figure does not include prisoners in Puerto Rico and in eight states that did not report age statistics.) In addition, over a hundred thousand juveniles were in some type of correctional care in 1985. The average age for federal prisoners was 32.2 years.

• *Being black or a member of another minority group.* In 1985, black Americans accounted for just over 12 percent of the country's total population. The nation's second-largest minority group, Hispanic (Spanish-speaking) Americans, made up about 6 percent of the total. In the federal prison system, though, 26.5 percent of inmates were black and 15.8 percent Hispanic. As for the states, in only one, Hawaii, are nonwhites in the majority. But fifteen states reported nonwhite prison majorities in 1985. (Four states—Colorado, Louisiana, Maine, and Wyoming—did not provide racial breakdowns.)

• *Coming from a city.* Today, as in the past, urban areas tend to produce more crimes, and more prisoners, than rural ones. In 1984, 53 percent of all Massachusetts inmates were from Boston and the communities immediately surrounding it.

• *Having a low income.* According to a study conducted in Boston in 1969, a low-income person (defined that year as anyone earning less than $75 a week—the figure would be higher now) was twice as likely to face a term in prison as one whose income came to more than $75 weekly. In all, "poor" defendants were convicted in 59 percent of cases, "nonpoor" ones in 40 percent, researchers found.

• *Being a school dropout.* Department of Corrections officials in Rhode Island say that 80 percent of the inmates they work with lack a high school diploma. Twenty-three percent are "functionally illiterate," which means they can read a few words but not enough to fill out a job application or understand the daily paper.

• *Having inadequate job skills.* Only 2 percent of those incarcerated in Massachusetts state prisons in 1984 had ever held a professional position. Of those in Rhode Island institutions, 40 percent had never held a steady job, that is, a job that lasted three months or more, of any kind.

• *Being addicted to drugs.* In Washington, D.C, over a quarter of all inmates are behind bars on drug-related charges. Eighty percent of the women incarcerated in Massachusetts have committed crimes connected to drug or alcohol abuse. Drugs are swelling prison populations today as alcohol did in the time of Prohibition.

An addict who is unprepared for a job and is ill educated, poor, urban, young, black, and male—that is the profile of a typical prisoner in many parts of the United States. Of course, there are exceptions to the rule. In states with small black populations—Idaho, Montana, North and South Dakota, and the states of northern New England—prisons are overwhelmingly white. Hawaii, with its large Oriental population, has prisons to match; 60 percent of Hawaiian prisoners were ethnic (national) Orientals in 1985. Alaska, not surprisingly, has a high percentage of Native American prisoners, and New Mexico's prisons are over 50 percent Hispanic. State-to-state variations in average prisoner age are evident as well, ranging from Nevada's high of thirty-one years to New Hampshire's low of twenty years. Women currently make up the fastest-growing segment of American prison populations, and teachers, lawyers, doctors, and corporate executives can be found among the imprisoned. Despite such exceptions, however, the nation's prisons remain lopsidedly young, poor, black, male, jobless, uneducated, and addicted. Why?

There are those who argue that the answer has to do with natural criminal tendencies. Young males from the nation's slums and racial ghettos are predisposed to crime, they maintain. Such people know no other way of life, nor do they care to. One man who has studied the relationship between crime and the slum, Edward C. Banfield, described the situation as he saw it: "A slum is not simply a district of low-quality housing. Rather it is one in which the style of life is squalid and vicious." Banfield wrote that statement after serving as head of a commission appointed in 1970 by President Richard M. Nixon to look into the crime-slum connection. The words come from Banfield's book *The Unheavenly City: The Nature and Future of the Urban Crisis,* in which he set forth some of the commission's findings.

The Unheavenly City outlines Banfield's view of the mind-set of "lower-class individual." He is "incapable of conceptualizing the future or of controlling his impulses . . . obliged to live from moment to moment . . . . impulse governs his behavior . . . . [he is] radically improvident. . . . His bodily needs (especially for sex) and his taste for 'action' take precedence over everything else." The slum dweller has no desire to work, a feeble sense of self, and a powerful drive to destroy and vandalize. "Features that make the slum repellent to others actually please him," Banfield concluded at one point.

Banfield's conviction that slums are voluntarily occupied by a born criminal class was not new in 1970. Exactly a century earlier, during the same convention of the Prison Congress at which Zebulon Brockway issued his plea for reform, delegates heard another speaker calling for a new awareness of the "criminal classes as such." Like Banfield, the 1870 speaker had firm ideas about the social and ethnic composition of those classes. Of the inmates he had studied at fifteen different American prisons, over half had been born outside the United States. Of those born here, half had parents who had emigrated from "the old country." The conclusion was inescapable: crime is the work of foreigners.

The identical theme was echoed almost forty years later in an article entitled "The Increase of Crime in the United States." Its author, one J. E. Brown, listed the types of people he took to be predisposed to violence: "The Italian bandit and the bloodthirsty Spaniard, the bad man from Sicily, the Hungarian, Croatian and the Pole, the Chinaman and the Negro, the Cockney Englishman, the Russian and the Jew, with all the centuries of hereditary hate back of them." Brown took care to alert his readers as to where they might expect to run into these dangerous types "huddled" together: "in the poorer quarters of our great cities."

To most of us today, descended as we are from Jews, Russians, Londoners, Poles, Italians, and the rest, Brown's words reek of racism and ethnic prejudice. For some, they may also cast new light on present-day assumptions about the "violent tendencies" of certain racial, social, and economic groups and create serious doubt as to the link that Banfield and others like him claim to have discovered between criminals and the slum.

Not that a link does not exist. It does, as the makeup of U.S. prison populations demonstrates. But is that link the result of the moral weakness and depravity of people who are "pleased" to live in the ghetto? Or has it been forged by slum conditions themselves, by hopeless poverty, run-down schools, welfare hotels, a lack of jobs, a flood of drugs, and, above all, by the desperate realization that there may be no escape? Such questions have no simple answers, but many would argue that it is slums, not slum dwellers, that breed crime and fill our jails and prisons with young black and Hispanic men and boys.

Some would argue that there is another reason that U.S. prison population statistics are skewed in the direction of the young, the black, the male, and the poor. This reason has to do with the way Americans perceive crime and distinguish among its many forms.

Say the word *crime* and what comes to mind? Murder. Robbery. Assault. Drug deals. Rape. Purse snatching. Mugging. Violence on a dark street.

Violence on a dark street. That about sums it up. The kind of crime uppermost in the minds of a majority of Americans is so-called street crime, violent street crime. That is the sort of crime people read about in the papers every morning and see each evening on the television news. They see and hear about street crime in television entertainment programming, too, and in the movies, and come across it in books and magazines and comics.

They hear about it and are entertained by it but they also

fear it. Public opinion polls indicate that the dread of becoming a street-crime victim is a number-one concern among Americans. Not only that, the polls show that a majority of citizens believe that such crime is increasing. Actually, 1986 figures from the U.S. Justice Department's Bureau of Justice Statistics indicated that violent crime was on the decrease. Ignoring the statistics, however, Americans have acted upon their conviction that crime is rising. Over the last decade, state after state has taken a "get-tough" approach toward criminals. This approach usually translates into longer and longer prison sentences for more and more of those found guilty of committing crimes.

Of committing *street* crimes. And who is likeliest to commit a street crime? Someone who has spent much of his life "on the street," particularly on a city street. Often that means a boy or man who has left school and cannot find a job. A man from the ghetto who is snared in poverty and perhaps by drugs as well. A young man impatient to possess the trappings of the good life—smart clothes, a car, a girlfriend to buy things for and impress. Someone who is desperate for money to feed a drug addiction. Someone, in other words, who is young, poor, black, male, and unequipped or unable to find or hold a good job. Someone who sees no other way of obtaining money than by stealing a wallet, holding up a liquor store, selling cocaine, or grabbing a necklace.

But street assaults and holdups are not the only kinds of crimes that occur in our society. There are scores of others. Hundreds of thousands of men and women fail to pay their full income tax each year, for instance. In 1986, just one tax dodger, Aldo Gucci, founder of the luxury leather-goods company, admitted to cheating the federal government out of $7 million. Dishonest employees embezzle far larger sums from banks and other businesses than are lost in robberies.

Computer experts have devised elaborate methods of diverting cash and squirreling it away in personal bank accounts halfway around the world. Americans forge checks and drive cars under the influence of liquor or other drugs. They steal from the companies they work for, walking off with everything from pens and paper clips to guns and chain saws. Early in 1987, officials at the U.S. Department of Defense estimated yearly losses due to theft there at $900 million. Industrialists authorize the illegal dumping of chemical wastes so toxic that they have poisoned entire neighborhoods and caused unknown numbers of illnesses and deaths. The heads of giant corporations increase their profits by selling faulty parts and equipment to the Defense Department. Defense officials knowingly pay exorbitant prices for those parts and equipment—and receive generous "kickbacks" for their trouble. Outright bribes are exchanged, too. Teachers infringe upon copyright laws when they reproduce pages from a text or workbook to hand out to a class of students. Copying without permission instead of buying the book amounts to stealing from the author and publisher. It's stealing when someone uses video cassette machines to duplicate a copyrighted movie.

But how many kids end up in prison because they illegally recorded a movie on the family VCR? How many teachers are deprived of their freedom because they stole an author's work? How many industrialists, bank officers, computer technicians, defense contractors and officials, and insurance salespeople are punished with prison sentences for stealing the billions of dollars that they pocket each year? How severe are the sentences they do get? Eighty-one-year-old Aldo Gucci was condemned to a year and a day in prison for his $7 million tax cheat. He was ordered to serve that term in a minimum-security facility with parole possible after just four months. By contrast, Charles Thornton (age twenty-five, black, of Washington, D.C.) was sentenced to a minimum of three years at a maximum security prison for possession with intent to distribute $40 worth of heroin. According to federal figures, the average sentence for anyone serving a term for robbery in a federal prison is thirty-seven months. For fraud, it's twenty-three months. Burglars serve an average of forty-seven months; embezzlers, twenty-two months. Only 60 percent of all white-collar criminals are sentenced to any time at all behind bars, and 80 percent get sentences of under a year. If American laws and American courts were as tough on white-collar criminals as they are on street criminals, prison populations would be a lot whiter, older, better educated and more gainfully employed, freer of drugs, and more suburban than they are now.

It's unlikely that prison populations will ever undergo such a change, though. That is partly because to most people, white-collar crime does not seem as serious as street crime. Certainly, white-collar crime costs this country a great deal of money. But it isn't scary the way street crime is. Being hit over the head and robbed of $50 is a painful, direct, and personal experience, one that will haunt the victim for weeks or months. Having to pay an extra $50 for groceries over the course of a year to help cover the losses inflicted by an embezzling executive, on the other hand, is indirect and impersonal. Customers may grumble about the high prices, but they won't feel the same way about paying them as they would about handing over a wallet at gunpoint. They may never even realize that they are paying extra, or why. Obviously, the supermarket is not going to advertise the facts.

That is another factor that tends to keep white-collar criminals out of prison. Their victims are less apt than the victims of street criminals to insist that charges be brought against them. Public and political attitudes readily accept non-prison sanctions for them.

Victims of street crimes are invariably frightened and angry about what has happened to them. That fear and anger makes them eager for revenge. Rarely does the person who has been mugged or robbed lose any time in calling the police and demanding an arrest. But for the victim of a white-collar crime, it is different. The owner of a grocery store may be too embarrassed to admit that a trusted employee, perhaps even a friend or relative, has been stealing. The president of a bank may conclude that attracting new depositors will be impossible if it becomes known that a teller has been siphoning off large sums of money. So the president or the grocer may fire the thief quietly and cover the loss without informing the police that a crime has taken place. Not all of the 50 percent of unreported crimes that PREAP cites are necessarily violent street crimes, after all.

A third reason that well-to-do, middle-aged white-collar offenders are better able than young urban blacks to stay out of prison is that they have more advantages along every step of the criminal-justice path. The possibility that the white-collar criminal's victims will cooperate in pretending that the crime never occurred is only one of them. Another is that they are often financially able to come to a settlement with their victims. The white-collar criminal is also likely to have the ability to raise bail. To whom is a judge more likely to grant bail—an eighteen-year-old with no money, no job, and an address in a slum, or a forty-five-year-old with a thriving law practice and a $500,000 house in the suburbs? To a suspected embezzler who has been fired and is unlikely to have the chance to repeat his crime, or to an accused mugger who will probably have to rob again the same day if he is to eat and—probably more important to him—get a drug fix?

Which of the four are more likely to be able to come up with the money if the judge does grant bail? Which is most likely to come up with bail on credit? Such a means of raising bail money is possible: in 1986, Morris County, New Jersey, was experimenting with allowing detainees to use their Visa and Mastercard credit cards to obtain bail. The answers to these questions are obvious and demonstrate why jails have been labeled the "poorhouses" of late twentieth-century America.

Getting out on bail confers advantages of its own—and not just the advantage of unsupervised living, either. Conditions in most U.S. jails are even worse than those in most prisons. People held there get little exercise or fresh air. The food is typical institution food—"starch and steam," as one inmate described it—and sanitary facilities, including opportunities to bathe and shower, may be limited. By the time the no-bail defendant has spent a year or more in jail awaiting trial, he or she is almost sure to appear physically unfit and not quite clean. What a contrast to the defendant who has spent the same year out on bail, working, eating well and bathing daily, swimming, sailing, golfing, and enjoying a normal family and social life. Which defendant is going to make a better impression on judge and jury when the trial does get underway? No wonder statistics have shown that "poor" defendants have twice the conviction rate of "nonpoor" ones.

In some cases, it is the experience of being in jail itself that lands an accused person in prison. Jail conditions can be so bad that a defendant will decide not to contest the charges but to plead guilty and get into a prison where there is more living space and better work, study, and recreation programs. Even someone who is aware of being innocent, or who seems to have a good chance of being acquitted, may choose prison over jail, U.S. corrections officials say. The white-collar defendant out on bail faces no such self-defeating choice.

Another advantage of white-collar criminals is the ability to plea-bargain their way to a short prison term or to no term at all. Plea bargaining is a process whereby the defendant admits to being guilty of a crime that is less serious than the one for which he or she was originally arrested. In return for the guilty plea (which saves the time and expense of a trial) government prosecutors ask the judge to impose a relatively light sentence.

One successful plea bargainer was LaMarr Hoyt, award-winning pitcher for baseball's San Diego Padres. Arrested in October 1986—his third arrest that year—in the act of smuggling illegal drugs into the country, Hoyt faced felony charges that could have netted him twenty years in prison and a half million dollars in fines. In an agreement with federal prosecutors, Hoyt pleaded guilty to two misdemeanor charges. His sentence: sixty days in a federal detention center, a fine of up to $5,000, five years of probation with regular drug testing, and forfeiture of the $33,000 sports car he used to transport the drugs.

What a deal! How did Hoyt manage to pull it off? A big part of the answer must be that he had good advice from a lawyer. Access to the nation's leading legal talents is another advantage the middle-class or corporate defendant has over the ordinary street criminal. It is true, of course, that every defendant charged with a felony has the right to be represented by an attorney in a court of law. This right has been set forth by the U.S. Supreme Court in a series of rulings dating back to the 1930s. The justices have even ruled that defendants who do not know a lawyer must have one provided for them. If a defendant cannot afford to pay the lawyer, the public foots the bill.

But being represented by a court-appointed attorney is one thing, and being represented by one's own personal lawyer, or better still, by a battery of them, is quite another. Most court-appointed lawyers are hardworking and conscientious, but they may be young or inexperienced in criminal proceedings. They may be juggling dozens of cases at the same time. Too often they seek to bargain for a lesser charge rather than following the more difficult course of defending the client's innocence. They work at a relatively low rate of pay—$20 to $40 an hour, perhaps, instead of $100 or more. Court-appointed lawyers are unlikely to know their clients well, if at all. They may not even speak the same language. In one headline-making case, a man who had arrived in the United States shortly before as a refugee from Southeast Asia was arrested on a murder charge. A judge named a lawyer to represent the man, but the lawyer could not understand when his client tried to explain that he was not the person the police thought they had arrested. The mixup went undiscovered until the trial was about to begin. And even then, the discovery of the man's identity was made not by the lawyer but by an employee of the court.

Having a clever lawyer who is devoted to a client's interests continues to be an advantage throughout a trial. Such a lawyer can introduce so many complications and delays that prosecutors may eventually conclude that the case is no longer worth pursuing. The best and most highly paid lawyers have the time, the funds, and the incentive to locate expert witnesses—doctors, psychiatrists, chemists, and others—with the ability to refute or cast doubt on the testimony of the experts called by the government side.

A good lawyer is an advantage after the trial, too, if there is a guilty verdict to be appealed. Under U.S. law, convicted criminals can appeal to a higher court if they believe that doing so may result in a ruling that the trial was unfair in some way or that a verdict was in error. Again, the defendant with money, influential friends, and good standing in the community has a better chance of making a successful appeal—and staying out of prison—than the average youth from the ghetto.

He or she has other advantages as well. An athlete who can afford a $33,000 car can probably also afford private treatment aimed at helping him overcome his drug problem. Private treatment is expensive; in the New York City area, it can cost up to $850 a day for a twenty-eight-day minimum. Money like that is beyond the reach of kids from the slums, who have to rely upon whatever publicly funded programs are open to them. Too often, none are, and prison is the only alternative. In mid-1986, 1,673 Washington, D.C., drug addicts were sitting in city jails awaiting places at crowded treatment centers. Another five hundred or so were waiting in federal facilities.

Other nonprison alternatives are more available to middle- and upper-income people than to lower-income people. The former are well able to support themselves and are less likely than the latter to be forced onto welfare if a judge grants them probation. They can provide for their families, too—that is, they can provide for them unless they are in prison. The desire to keep a white-collar criminal's family off the welfare rolls has prompted many a judge to substitute probation for a prison term. Such a desire may not be operative in the case of an impoverished slum dweller. Judges are likely to assume that his family will be on relief whether he's in prison or out of it.

Another alternative to prison is being sentenced to provide a service to the community. Such community work might come in the form of teaching academic subjects to school dropouts, offering vocational training, or giving free professional advice—legal, medical, or financial, for example—to those who cannot afford to pay for it. Clearly, white-collar and corporate offenders, with their education, experience, and ability to make a genuine contribution to society, are more likely than street criminals to be sentenced to community service instead of prison.

Finally, a white-collar crime is more likely than a street crime to carry a penalty that is in itself an alternative to incarceration. A jail or prison cell is the traditional destination of anyone convicted of a crime of violence. But whoever heard of an industrialist being imprisoned for dumping chemical pollutants into a lake or river? At most, the polluter's company may be slapped with a fine. One clear-cut example of the distinction our society makes between a "rich man's crime" and a "poor man's crime" is contained in the federal immigration law passed by Congress in 1986. Congress designed this law to cut down on illegal immigration, especially by young Latin Americans who secretly enter the United States in search of jobs. Among the law's provisions: any employer who hires an illegal alien can be fined—$250 to $2,000 for the first offense, $2,000 to $5,000 for the second offense, and so forth. But the illegal aliens who allow themselves to be hired can be fined $2,000 for the first offense *and* sent to prison for up to two years. The result of this law can only be a further tilt in prison populations in the direction of the young, the poor, and the Hispanic.

This law is not the only crime bill that Congress has passed in the 1980s. Another was the Comprehensive Crime Control Act of 1984. According to its supporters, that act will bring a greater degree of fairness and uniformity into criminal sentencing and punishment on the federal level.

One type of unfairness tackled by the Crime Control Act was that brought about by older laws that allowed federal judges wide latitude in deciding how severe a sentence to impose. Under these laws, a judge might be able to hand down a sentence ranging anywhere from ten to twenty years. Or from fifteen years to life. Or from probation to ten years. Depending upon how a judge felt about a particular crime, and about a particular criminal, he or she might give out a maximum sentence—or one that barely covered the minimum. Two people of the same age and background, living in the same neighborhood and standing convicted of the same type of crime, could receive sentences that differed enormously in length.

The 1984 act addressed this kind of discrepancy with a plan for uniform sentencing in federal courtrooms. The plan called for a numerical system to be used to determine exact punishments. Responsibility for working out the details of the system was placed in the hands of a seven-member U.S. Sentencing Commission.

Two years later, in the fall of 1986, the commission issued its preliminary 170-page report. An amended report was submitted to Congress the next spring and its recommendations went into effect in late 1987. The new rules list approximately 2,600 separate criminal offenses and ranks each according to how seriously it is regarded. For example, the crime of assault with intent to murder might carry a sentence of anywhere from 33 to 41 months in prison.

Rarely, however, is the crime considered by itself. Other factors are taken into account, and each of these factors can end up adding to the sentence. More time is tacked on to the original sentence for aggravating circumstances—for example, if the criminal is a repeat offender or used a gun. Additional time is piled on if the victim has been permanently injured. When the length of the sentence has been determined in this way, it is mandatory for the judge to impose that sentence. Only if the judge feels strongly that the sentence would be inappropriate in a particular instance may he or she alter the punishment. In that case, the judge must file a written explanation.

Another inconsistency with which the 1984 act attempted to deal involves parole. For years, many Americans have been critical of parole. It makes a mockery of the idea of punishing criminals by depriving them of their freedom, critics say. Justice Department figures show that as of the mid-1980s, only 16 percent of state and federal prisoners were serving their full sentences. Most were serving less than half. A second criticism of parole is that the system is too open to manipulation by prisoners and prison authorities alike. It is not right, many Americans believe, for one prisoner to be able to wangle his way to freedom while another, convicted of the same type of crime and with a similar prison record, is kept behind bars for the maximum term.

The Crime Act of 1984 therefore mandated an eventual end to parole for federal prisoners and scheduled it to be phased out in the early 1990s. In place of parole will be a renewed emphasis on the system whereby prisoners are rewarded for good behavior by having their sentences reduced by as much as fifty-four days for each year served.

Since the Comprehensive Crime Control Act is a federal law, its provisions apply only to prisoners in the federal system. With its passage, though, Justice Department officials began urging state legislatures to adopt similar no-parole and uniform-sentencing rules.

Would an end to parole and the use of uniform sentencing mean a criminal-justice system that is fairer on the federal level, and perhaps eventually on the state, county, and local levels, as well? Not everyone is convinced of it. The doubters point out that ending parole could have some unexpected ill effects. Parole was a reform to begin with, they remind us, instituted in response to the fact that fixed sentences gave prisoners no motive to try to improve themselves. In Maine, where parole was abolished in 1976, the warden of the state prison at Thomaston feels that his job has become more difficult as a result. "There really are guys that know they're going to be here the rest of their life," he says, and knowing that makes them all the more uncaring and hard to handle. Defenders of no-parole respond that a fifty-four-day-per-year reduction for good behavior is incentive enough for prisoner cooperation.

But the critics have other grounds for their objection to ending parole. Granting early releases had become one way of reducing prison overcrowding. No more parole is going to mean fuller and fuller prisons, they warn, and the more overcrowded a prison, the more vulnerable it may be to unrest and rioting. At the same time, overcrowding forces cutbacks in education and job-training programs and in counseling and other services intended to ease a convict's way back into society. Doing away with parole will hurt both prisoners and prisons themselves, some believe. New York State, at one time scheduled to phase out parole in 1985, reversed itself and decided to retain the system.

Some critics also see problems resulting from uniform sentencing. Everyone agrees that compelling judges to hand out fixed terms will mean more criminals getting longer sentences. Again, overcrowding will result. In Washington, D.C., jail terms have been mandatory for convicted drug dealers since 1983. Jail populations have soared, yet the number of drug sales being made on Washington streets has not dropped. In fact, it has risen dramatically since 1983. Mandatory sentencing has had no deterrent effect on drug dealing in the nation's capital, but it *has* filled jails there to the point where judges order prisoner releases on the grounds that the overcrowding produces conditions that amount to cruel and unusual punishment. To avoid such court-ordered releases, D.C. prosecutors get around the law by permitting many of those arrested on drug charges to plea-bargain their way to freedom on a charge for which the law does not demand a prison sentence. Ignoring the law's mandate, judges routinely impose alternative sentences. In Washington, at least, fixed sentencing has created more problems than it has solved. It will do the same elsewhere, many caution. Testifying before New Jersey legislators in 1986, the state's attorney general predicted that if the lawmakers voted to go ahead with a plan for mandatory prison sentences for drug peddlers, it would cost $2 billion to build enough cells to hold all the convicted.

Finally, the critics worry that the Comprehensive Crime Control Act's effort to end unfairness in the criminal justice system may be fundamentally misdirected. The effect of the act is to even out sentencing and punishment for those men and women who end up convicted of a crime and headed for prison. Fair enough. But the law ignores a greater inequity in the system—the inequity that sends a disproportionate percentage of street criminals to courtrooms, jails, and prison while allowing white-collar and corporate lawbreakers overwhelming advantages all the way through the unfolding of the process of justice.

Defenders of the act argue that Congress did attempt to redress this inequity. The act does make provision for dealing more severely with some forms of business crime. Under it, such offenses as trademark violations, credit card fraud, computer crime, arson for profit, and murder for hire have become federal crimes. This is a step in the right direction, critics of the act agree, but not a big enough step. The most important and talked-about sections of the new law are those that concern parole and uniform sentencing, and both are just one more "get-tough" approach to street crime. That approach, the critics believe, has been largely responsible for making our prisons the ineffective and problem-filled places they are today.

Another suggestion for reforming the sentencing process is to allow the victim of a crime to have a say in what happens to the defendant. Some crime victims argue that permitting them to participate in decisions regarding bail and the severity of the sentence is only fair. They should also be consulted about possible probation or parole, they say. One who advocates this idea is Louise Gilbert, mother and mother-in-law of two 1981 murder victims. "The parents, spouse and children of a murder victim are victims too," she contends, "and their willingness to become involved should be shored up with legislation and changes in court practice." She urged such changes and new laws in a 1984 article in *Newsweek* magazine. Victims "should be consulted about charges, plea bargains and tactics," she wrote.

But others are leery of victim participation in sentencing. In 1983, Angola State Prison inmate Wilbert Rideau, whom we met in Chapter 2, coauthored an article on that subject in *The Angolite*. In the article, he and fellow-prisoner Billy Sinclair contended that this practice threatens to undermine justice rather than to enhance it. Rideau and Sinclair cited instances in which pressure from victims and their families and friends has resulted in judges' altering the sentences they originally imposed. Such pressure is "designed to control and intimidate the justice system rather than make it function properly and equitably," the two maintained. In 1987, the U.S. Supreme Court ruled that the mental suffering inflicted upon crime victims and their families cannot be taken into account in sentencing.

Will victim participation be a part of criminal sentencing

in the future? Will uniform sentencing and reduced reliance upon parole transform our system of sentencing and make it fairer to all? Some predict it will; others disagree. But whatever happens, one thing is certain: For the convicted, the handing down of a sentence of imprisonment marks the start of a grim new way of life.

5

In Prison

The room, about the size of a large classroom, is slightly grimy and utterly bare of decoration. Twenty or so metal chairs form a rough circle in the center. An old wooden table is pushed against one wall. On it stand a coffeemaker and a pile of Styrofoam cups. The curtainless windows are covered with thick wire mesh. They are open, but the radiators are hissing, and the room, on this mild October evening, is steamingly hot.

Singly or in groups of two or three, the women enter. The first to arrive looks about forty-five. She is wearing a lime green sweat suit, and dark hair hangs limply around her pale face. When she speaks, her open mouth reveals that several teeth are missing. Following her is a plump black woman in her twenties dressed in slacks and a cotton shirt. Then comes a young white woman, a light-skinned black woman in tightly belted khaki, and two women who drag their chairs aside and whisper together in Spanish. Others drift in slowly. Last of all to take her seat is a tall, sophisticated-looking girl in her late teens. She wears a designer outfit and fashionable boots. Her

71

stylishly cut hair shines blonde under the harsh ceiling lights, and her smile gives every indication of being the product of years of expensive orthodontia. Settling herself, crossing her legs, and adjusting her collar with long, graceful fingers, this girl looks the very image of a student at an exclusive prep school or college.

She's not, though. She, like her drabber companions, is a prisoner, an inmate in a state correctional institution for female criminals. Like them, she has come to this room to talk, to take part in a program designed to encourage prisoners to discuss their feelings and concerns in order to reach a better understanding of themselves and their lives. Also present is the social worker who helped establish this program four or five years ago and still serves as chairperson of its advisory board; the woman hired to run the program on a day-by-day basis; a criminal-justice professor who acts as adviser to the program; a program volunteer whose job it is to help guide the conversation; and a writer. *Not* present is any C.O. or other prison official. Allowing prisoners to meet without a C.O. is unusual, but the aim of this program is to get the women to talk with complete openness and honesty. Here in this room, for two hours one night a week, the women know that nothing they say will be reported to the authorities or used against them.

Although the prisoners have gathered to talk, conversation is slow to get underway. The woman in green—call her "Sherrie"—jumps up to fill coffee cups and offer powdered milk and sugar. "Sissie," the one in khaki, leaves and returns with an electric fan. At a suggestion from "Bunny," the plump black woman, two groups form, smokers on one side of the circle and nonsmokers on the other. The ten or twelve prisoners all choose the smoking side; the visitors alone are nonsmokers.

"Who wants to lead?" the program director asks. Sherrie doesn't hesitate. "I will. You see that movie on TV last night? About the mother that was beating on her kids? Wasn't that great?" The others nod. Most of them did see the movie, but Sherrie cannot be stopped from retelling the plot anyway. It haunts her. She describes how her mother abused her, and again, most of the other women nod. Having been the victim of an abusive parent is one experience that nearly all share.

There are others. Every prisoner in the room, it becomes clear, has a drug or alcohol problem. Some stole to support a habit, and some committed assault. (Since this group is limited to "short-termers," those serving sentences of five years or less, it is unlikely that anyone here has committed a crime as serious as manslaughter or murder. A separate, similar program is offered for the prison's "long-termers.") Another bond among the women is that nearly all have worked on the street as prostitutes. Most are mothers, although only Sherrie refers directly to her daughter. "I don't know where she is now," she says matter-of-factly. "My mother used to have her; then she went with her stepmother. She's fourteen; I had her when I was fifteen." It's a shock to realize that this worn, haggard woman is not yet thirty years old. The years in prison and on the street have taken their toll on Sherrie, as they have on most of the others. All but one or two of this group are repeat offenders with criminal records stretching back to their early teens, and the majority have spent time in prison before. As they talk, their words weave a vivid picture of their lives behind bars.

It's a picture set against an ugly background, the physical structure of the prison itself. The main building at this facility dates back over a hundred years. Like the dozens of other nineteenth-century state and federal prisons still in use, it was designed as a fortress, inside and out. High ceilings, deep stairwells, bare floors, and lots of wood and metal add up to an atmosphere that threatens to overwhelm ordinary human feelings. Natural daylight hardly penetrates the long hallways and dark-paneled rooms. Voices echo, and every sound— steps in the corridor, banging doors, the creaks and groans of ancient plumbing and heating systems—is so magnified that it becomes difficult to hear what anyone else is saying. Even across this small circle, words and sentences must be repeated over and over.

Sissie talks about what it is like to be a prisoner in this building. She has spent time here in the institution's maximum-security wing—"max," she calls it. The cells are small and dingy, and it's noisy. "Someone screaming all the time." Who? "One of the crazies." The state's female criminally insane are sent to max because there is no separate facility for them. Another section of the wing, "max-max," contains the cells used for solitary confinement. Women are condemned to stretches in solitary for such major infractions of the rules as fighting or smuggling drugs in from outside. Under state law, an inmate can be kept in solitary no longer than fifteen days. After one day out, however, she may be sent back for further punishment. In some prisons in this state, inmates have been confined in solitary for over a year at a time.

Living conditions in other U.S. prisons are just as grim— if not more so. At the men's maximum-security facility in a neighboring state, inmates live in tiny cagelike cells arranged in rows three tiers high. The men's prison was built in 1878, just two years after General George Custer and his troops fell at Little Bighorn. A series of metal stairs and narrow catwalks link the tiers, and the pounding of footsteps, the deep echoes of male voices, and the clang of metal striking metal seem unending. The prisoners have no way of shutting out the sounds, for their cells have no doors, only barred gates. Nor

74

are they able to shut out the sights of prison. Dim lights burn day and night on each cell block, enabling C.O.s to keep the men under constant surveillance.

In some ways, conditions are even worse in the same prison's medium-security unit. There each prisoner is assigned to sleep on a cot in a huge dormitory, and that cot represents his only personal space. Whereas the men in max can individualize their cells—usually by taping *Playboy*-type photos to the walls—those in the dorm can't do even that much. And while those in the cells have room to store their own clothes and a few personal possessions, the ones in the dorm are limited to what can be contained in a small footlocker. That means, among other things, that the men cannot keep their own clothing but must wear prison-issue items at all times. So barren are conditions in the dorm, one prison official laments, that many inmates would rather stay in max than be "promoted" to medium-security status.

The women's prison has a dorm unit, too. Sherrie, Sissie, and the rest hate it as the men do theirs. All the women in the room have spent time in the dorm, because it is there that newly arrived inmates stay while they await classification and a cell assignment. Others in the dorm include women who have been sentenced to very short terms—a few days for drunk driving, for example. The dormitory building contains fifty cots, each with a locker at its foot, marching in precise rows up and down one long room. A wall-mounted television mutters softly in the corner by the door. Half a dozen women stare dully at a game show, squirming restlessly in hard, straight-backed chairs. Directly behind the glass-walled C.O. s' room is the building's only bathroom, containing a shower, a sink, a washing machine, and six or seven toilets. There are no doors in the bathroom, and no toilet stalls. Anything that goes on there is clearly visible to any C.O. or visitor of either sex who happens to glance in its direction. This indignity is the cause of deep resentment among the women.

But the prisoners gathered in this discussion room tonight have already finished their time in the dorm, and none is currently in max. For them, conditions are more agreeable, on the surface at least. They live in various "cottages" scattered across the landscaped campus that surrounds the main prison building.

The cottages are relatively small, low buildings. Several are fronted with flower gardens planted and cared for by the inmates. All have lounges with bookshelves (but few books), a row of windows, a television, chairs or a couch, and a table. Each cottage has forty-odd rooms, some with bunk beds for two inmates, a few with a cot for only one. The tiny rooms have one window apiece, and besides beds, all are equipped with a doorless closet, a bureau, and a sink and toilet.

The women are permitted to fix up their rooms. One of them, "home" to a white-haired long-termer named "Mimi," is actually charming. Lacy curtains cover the window, almost disguising the fact that it is really no window at all, just a heavily louvered affair that lets in a bit of light on a bright day. The cot is neatly made up with a bedspread and decorative pillows, and baskets hanging on a wall lend a homey touch. A small television perches on the edge of the bureau. Prisoners housed in the cottages at this institution, unlike those at some others, may have personal radios and TVs, but the sets must arrive in their original, unopened cartons directly from the store or manufacturer. There's a reason for the rule: prison officials know that families and friends may try to smuggle something—usually illegal drugs—to an inmate by slipping the contraband in among a set's circuitry. The suitability of televisions for smuggling purposes also makes repairs a problem. If Mimi's breaks down, she will probably not be allowed to send it to her family to be fixed but will have to order a whole new set. Rules meant to keep contraband out of prison explain another of Mimi's decorating touches: the dried flowers that fill a vase next to the television. Once she might have had a live houseplant, but these were outlawed after routine searches revealed that prisoners were burying packets of drugs in the soil.

Attractive as Mimi has made her room, an oppressive feeling still lingers about it. She, as much as the women in their dormitory and the men on a nineteenth-century cell block, is a prisoner. For her, too, the lights never go off. Because Mimi lives in an "honor" cottage, she has a key to her room, but that key works only in the small, light lock intended to keep her belongings safe from other prisoners. The heavy main lock—the gang lock—is controlled by an officer in the C.O.s' station across from the lounge. The gang lock is used mainly at night, although the officers can shut Mimi out of her cell, or into it, at any moment, for any length of time.

As it happens, Mimi and the others in her cottage were locked out only this morning. Acting on a tip that someone in the cottage had successfully smuggled some contraband, the C.O.s moved in before dawn and ordered everyone out of bed and into the lounge. The women went in nightgowns and pajamas—no bathrobes or other cover-ups allowed. Each was stripped and searched, and the rooms were gone over with a fine-tooth comb. If anything illegal came to light, Mimi knows nothing about it. Or so she claims.

Living the way they do, Mimi and her fellow prisoners have little sense of privacy. In a way, prison inmates become public property. Like animals in a zoo, they may be stared at, speculated about, and discussed before their very faces. Accompanied by a C.O. or prison official, any visitor can talk to Mimi and question her, and if Mimi fails to act meek and polite, she will find herself in trouble. At a word from the warden, the visitor can walk into Mimi's cell, even when Mimi isn't there, and look at her most intimate possessions. In fact, it isn't even necessary to go inside. An eye-level window set into the door keeps Mimi's cell, and Mimi herself, always on view. Only the toilet is out of sight through this window, but Mimi knows that if the C.O.s become suspicious about the amount of time she spends there, one of them will burst in to check on her. Mimi has managed to improve upon her surroundings, but nothing she can do will change them.

From talk about living conditions, the women in the group go on to discuss other aspects of prison life. Again Sherrie takes the lead, this time with a gripe about work assignments.

In general, prisoners in this country are required to work. Convicted prisoners, that it is. People awaiting trial in jails or detention centers cannot be compelled to keep busy. Criminals who have been found guilty and are serving their sentences in county or local jails, on the other hand, must do the jobs assigned to them. For the most part, these jobs, like prison jobs, are housekeeping chores: helping with food preparation, doing prison laundry, sweeping and cleaning, caring for the grounds, and the like. The kind of job a prisoner ends up doing depends upon his or her classification. A man classed as violent and kept in a maximum-security unit may find himself scrubbing floors in that unit. Outdoor work, or any work that removes a prisoner from surveillance, will be reserved for those in less-secure units. But whatever a prisoner's classification, he or she must do some job, unless a physical or mental disability makes that impossible.

"Well, I don't." Sherrie's tone is defiant. "I told them, I just won't work. And I don't." The others look skeptical, plainly regarding Sherrie's bragging words as a lie.

"You know what they pay you?" Sherrie presses on. "You

know the *most* they let you earn? A lousy $2.50 a week."

"It's really $5.00," the program director interjects. At a question from one of the visitors, she explains that half of everything prisoners in this state earn goes into a fund to be turned over to them when they are released.

"But $2.50 a week!" Sherrie won't give up. "That buys a couple packs of cigarettes." Since Sherrie has smoked and given away close to a pack in the last hour alone, it is obvious that she needs more than $2.50 a week to keep her going. She seems to have a point about the wages, too. In this state, prisoners earn anywhere from 13¢ to 62¢ an hour for work they are forced to perform. That does seem low.

Compared to what some other states pay their prisoners, it's generous. Colorado pays from 3¢ to 5¢ an hour; Oregon from 13¢ to $38¢; New Hampshire from 11¢ to 29¢. Five states—Georgia, Mississippi, Texas, Virginia, and Washington—reported paying their convicts nothing at all for doing prison jobs in 1985. The states with the highest maximum hourly wages that year included Minnesota (14¢ to $2), North Carolina (40¢ to $1), and Tennessee (50¢ to $1). The highest wages of all were in Arkansas. Inmates there could earn anywhere from $3.35 to $7.00 an hour.

Can Sherrie really get away with not working? "No," Bunny warns. "They won't let you. You'll get written up."

"You got written up, didn't you, Sissie?" the volunteer asks, trying to get the focus off Sherrie and onto someone else. "Wasn't your hearing today? How did it go?"

Sissie shrugs. "I go to lock-in tomorrow. Eight days." She sounds casual as she tells the story.

A couple of weeks ago, Sissie refused to obey an order from one of the C.O.s. She hardly remembers what it was: go there; come here; pick that up. It was the officer's tone and manner, not her words, that infuriated Sissie. "She don't have

79

to be so rude. I'm as good as her. I told her I won't do it." At that, the C.O. wrote up a disciplinary report, a D-report, and Sissie was scheduled for a hearing before the prison's disciplinary board. "I could of had a lawyer," she says, "but . . ." She shrugs again. "I talk for myself."

Her talk was apparently not very effective, and the board upheld the C.O.'s complaint. At lights-out tonight, the main lock on Sissie's cell will be closed by the officer at the desk, and it will be kept closed for the next eight days. Sissie will be allowed three books and some writing materials in her cell and taken out for a shower once a day. She will have one change of clothing and no TV. She is nonchalant about the prospect. "I'll sleep," she says. "And go on a diet." At one visitor's puzzled look, Sissie explains that while she's locked in, a C.O. will regularly push a tray of prison food through an opening in the bottom of her cell door. "I wouldn't eat that crap," she says scornfully. (Actually, she uses a stronger word. The women's talk is full of obscenities.) "I get my food at the commissary."

"Me too. Some weeks I spend $40." This from a white woman named "Laura" who has not spoken until now. Like Sherrie, Laura is pasty-complexioned and lacking a number of teeth. "You can get anything there." Laura exaggerates, but a visit to the prison store does prove it to be surprisingly well stocked. Not just snacks and cigarettes, but cans, jars, and packages of bread, peanut butter, soup, flour, and sugar line the shelves behind the counter. Meat is available from a freezer in the back room. The women who buy food here prepare it in the cottages' compact kitchens. They do all their cooking on top of the stoves, even managing to bake cakes and cookies there, because the ovens have been disconnected. Food is stored in each kitchen's refrigerator, a refrigerator that the C.O.s keep locked to reduce pilferage. Not everyone

80

in the prison gets to cook for herself, though. The women in the dorm don't, and neither do those in max or the Awaiting Trial Unit. And women cannot cook food they don't have, either. Unless their families are willing and able to send them money for the commissary, they will be stuck with prison fare. It seems to be as much of an advantage to be "rich" in a twentieth-century American prison as it was eight hundred years ago in an English jail.

Prisoners are not entirely dependent upon their families for cash, however. In all but five states, they have the wages, minuscule though they are, from their prison jobs. Besides that, some may find work in a prison industry.

Most prisons have industrial programs. In general, these are aimed at providing goods for the institution itself or for the state. The women in this prison, for instance, produce clothing for themselves and for other prisoners. Flags are often made in prison workshops, and so are the official decals that identify state-owned vehicles and other property. "It's almost funny," comments an official in one state, "to see all these prisoners turning out all those symbols of freedom." The manufacture of automobile license plates is another standard prison job. In New York, a few female inmates serve the state Department of Motor Vehicles by answering telephones and responding to questions about drivers' licenses and auto registration. In Delaware, inmate work crews have completed two new prison facilities, one in Smyrna and the other near Georgetown. From place to place, prison industries also furnish food items to various state institutions, produce goods that can be sold for a profit, or supply labor for private businesses. Prison contract labor now is different from that of the past; today's prisoners remain in the institution and fulfill their contract obligations there, and the institution continues to be responsible for their care and discipline.

Prison industries can be profitable for the facilities that run them. In 1986, the California Prison Industry Authority announced a record $52 million worth of production during the previous year. After costs, this boiled down to a saving of $15 million, according to the state's Department of Corrections. The Delaware construction program saved that state $25 million, or so corrections authorities claimed. At the same time, the industries are supposed to benefit the inmates. According to those who direct the programs, industry jobs keep prisoners busy, teach them a trade, and allow them to earn more money than they could merely by doing their assigned prison tasks.

Does it really work out that way? Most prisoners, including the ones in the women's discussion group, say it does not. A visit to their sewing room helps explain why they feel that way.

This large, dismal room in the prison's old main building is equipped in a manner that seems to match the building in age. The machinery looks more like part of an exhibit of nineteenth-century factory life than like anything one would expect to see in a modern workplace. An inmate could spend ten years becoming an expert on one of these antiques and wind up not much better qualified for sewing or mill work than she was to begin with. So much for meaningful job training. In some prisons, equipment is just one problem. The jobs that inmates learn are not necessarily jobs that will be open to them in the outside world. Men trained to make license plates, for instance, protest that since the plates are made only in prison, they are being prepared for jobs they will have to return to prison to do!

As far as keeping prisoners busy is concerned, this sewing room, at least, seems to be a flop. One woman leans on a sewing machine, slowly sipping coffee and gazing into space.

Across from her, another puffs smoke rings into the already-hazy atmosphere. At the back of the room, two inmates lean against a table with a C.O. between them. The three laugh and chat together like the best of buddies. Only one woman is doing anything that could be described as work. Fingers moving at a snail's pace, she picks crooked stitches from a pair of work pants. There must be times when this shop, and the others in the industrial wing, hum with activity—the state's prisoners are adequately supplied with clothing, after all—but this is not such a day.

One reason for the women's lethargy could have to do with the wages they are getting. Fifty cents to $1 an hour—that's the rate of pay for prison industries in this state. For contract piecework—a job such as pulling plastic tabs off metal disks for a private company that will use the disks in a manufacturing process—the rate of pay is 1¢ per disk. Again, the pay scale is lower elsewhere: 15¢ to 25¢ an hour in Alabama; 6¢ to 14¢ an hour in Indiana; 5¢ to 11¢ an hour in Virginia; nothing at all in Mississippi, Georgia, and Texas. Delaware prison-building inmates worked from dawn to dusk—for 50¢ a day. How, indignant prisoners demand, can anyone expect them to do their best work for such measly wages? Or for no wage at all? Why should they sign up to perform a tiresome, repetitious chore for a fraction of the pay a free-world employee would get for doing the same work? "A hundred disks—$1," Mimi says in disgust, explaining why the prison is having trouble finding women to fill this particular contract. How, at such a rate of pay, does anyone expect prisoners to come away with the feeling that doing a job well brings financial reward and personal satisfaction? Are they being motivated to look for jobs after they are released? Inmates also complain about unsafe conditions in many prison workshops. Such conditions would be against the law in the outside world, they contend. Altogether, prison industries are a sore spot with inmates in most institutions around the country, with most prisoners convinced that the industries exist to profit the state at their expense.

Even some prison authorities concede that their industrial programs are far from perfect. To the problems cited by prisoners, they add that the programs are not extensive enough. Too often, jobs are unavailable to those who, despite the drawbacks and the low pay, want them. Massachusetts officials, while aiming to employ 40 percent of their prisoners, recorded an actual employment level of 9.1 percent in 1985. Such a work rate must leave prisoners with a lot of time on their hands.

"What do you do?" one of the visitors to the women's prison asks the discussion group. "After your tasks are done, if you can't get work in the industries, what do you do all day?" As usual, Sherrie is ahead of everyone else with her answer: "Sleep." If Sherrie is to be believed—and the women are looking doubtful again—she spends eighteen or twenty hours a day in bed.

The other women would be bored by such an existence, and they find something to do to pass the time—watch television, mostly. Many Americans are critical of all the TV viewing that goes on in prison. It spoils the prisoners, they say. Prison authorities disagree. Whether or not they allow TV and radios in individual cells, few would eliminate it in lounges or recreation rooms. Television might have been a luxury twenty-five or thirty years ago, one warden explains, but today it's a necessary means of control. Without it, prisoners would be even more restless and trouble-prone than they are now. It's also a way to keep inmates in touch with changes in the outside world.

Other forms of recreation are available to prisoners. U.S.

prisons are theoretically required to allow inmates an hour or more of outdoor exercise each day, although many are unable to meet this requirement in practice. On weekends, there may not be enough C.O.s on duty to watch the prisoners if they do go out. The weather may not cooperate. Logistics may get in the way. The administrator of Wiscasset, Maine's, Lincoln County Jail, for instance, has responsibility for only twenty prisoners, but these include adults and juveniles of both sexes. Since the law says that the sexes must be kept apart, and that underage prisoners may not set eyes on adult inmates, trying to get the various groups to and from the outdoor courtyard is an almost impossible "juggling act." Larger institutions, unlike this jail, have indoor gyms to provide more recreational opportunities. Some have poolrooms and weight-lifting facilities, which are becoming increasingly popular in both men's and women's prisons. Unfortunately, prison overcrowding means that prisoners' use of such facilities must be severely limited. On rare occasions, inmates may have the chance to see a play or a show put on by an outside group. Even more rarely, they may organize an entertainment of their own.

Attending classes is another way to fill in the time. The classes may be vocational: cooking, horticulture, typing, and computing are some of the skills the women in the discussion group can learn while serving their "bits"—sentences. In men's prisons, vocational classes typically include auto body work, carpentry, and barbering. Another kind of instruction that is increasingly being made available to prisoners concerns infant care and child rearing. Fathers and mothers enrolled in prison child-care classes receive more-frequent-than-usual visits from their children. Under the watchful eye of teachers and volunteers, they learn how to pick up a baby gently, offer toys to a toddler, be patient with a boisterous six-year-old, and communicate with a reluctant teenager. Such skills are alien to adults who were themselves frightened, battered, and neglected children only a few years before. In some parenting programs, hands-on training is supplemented by workshops in which prisoners discuss their own childhood and try to come up with ways to improve and strengthen their ties with the next generation.

Other prison classes are academic. The basic thrust of prison education is teaching illiterates to read and write, although prisoners capable of going beyond the basics can study for high school equivalency exams or master specific subjects like U.S. history or algebra. A very few even take college-level courses. At the women's prison, two inmates are on the verge of receiving their Associate of Arts degrees, having completed two years of learning under the auspices of a local community college.

Its classroom wing is one of the most cheerful areas of this entire facility. Perhaps because schools are themselves institutions, this school does not look remarkably different from any other. Pleasant teachers in civilian dress work diligently with their pupils. No officers are in evidence. The classrooms are outfitted with posters, blackboards, desks, tables, and rows of books. In one, two inmates crowd close to the teacher's desk, intent on a series of reading flashcards. In another, a slim black woman sits, legs curled about the rungs of her chair, books spread before her, writing a term paper. "She's one smart girl," the principal says proudly. One of the almost-college-graduates comes down the hall, and the visitors express admiration for her hard work. The woman smiles, but she has a problem she needs their help to solve. It is the type of problem that plagues even the best-intentioned of prison education programs.

The woman's sentence is nearly up, and she is due for a

transfer to a prerelease center. She told the authorities that she needed to go to a center in this part of the state in order to finish the two months remaining of her college classes. But the authorities did not understand, or did not remember, or there was some bureaucratic mix-up. Whatever it was, the woman heard last week that she's been assigned to a center over a hundred miles to the west, making it impossible for her to continue her classes and threatening to cost her several credits. What a choice: step toward freedom or a college degree. So far, the woman is choosing the degree—and extra time in prison—but she begs one of the visitors to intervene with the authorities on her behalf.

Other problems assail prison education programs. A prime one is the shortage of both teachers and money. The state has more than nine thousand jail and prison inmates and an education staff of sixty-two full-timers and eighty-five part-timers. This staff includes not only teachers but counselors, diagnosticians, and administrators. The yearly prison education budget from all sources comes to under $2.5 million.

Low pay and difficult working conditions contribute to yet another problem. Teachers in the system tend to resign after only a short time on the job, and when someone is not available to teach a particular academic or vocational course, that course is dropped. Among the women in the discussion group, it is "Pamela," the preppy-looking one, who is most bitter about the lack of course offerings. "Last time I was in," she says, daintily picking a bit of tobacco from her lip, "I took an electronics course and kept busy all the time. Now the teacher's gone, and there's nothing to do but horticulture. Somehow—" she shudders—"I don't see myself working in a garden all winter."

Pamela's frustration over the boredom of prison life is clear. She reads a lot, she says, borrowing books from the prison library, but a person can't read all the time. Pamela could, if she wanted to, also avail herself of the prison's separate law library (every jail and prison in the country is required to provide its population with legal references), turning herself into a legal expert and learning to manage her own court appeals. Many U.S. prisoners have done just that, and some have become competent "jailhouse lawyers," bringing suits aimed at shortening their terms or improving prison conditions for themselves or others.

But Pamela has no interest in the law and none in the institution's current educational and vocational offerings. When she is not deep in a romantic novel, watching television, or doing assigned work, she goes to discussions like this one, or to Alcoholics Anonymous or Narcotics Anonymous meetings. Not, she emphasizes, that she's trying to kick her own drug habit. The meetings provide a break in the routine, that's all. Pamela's so-what attitude about her admitted need for drugs somehow suggests that she may be getting an occasional supply from outside. She certainly claims to have smuggled enough drugs in to boyfriends while they were in prison, and she and Sherrie vie with each other in demonstrating how to pin drug-filled balloons to underclothing so as to escape the notice of all but the most vigilant of C.O.s.

Of course, hiding drugs in underwear will not work if the C.O. decides on a strip search, but even such searches, the women insist, are not enough to keep all drugs out of prison. Prison authorities agree, reluctantly admitting that not only visitors but some corrupt C.O.s as well slip drugs and alcohol to certain inmates. The fact that not even their own staff is to be fully trusted makes prison officials suspicious of everyone. In order to take part in this discussion program tonight, each of the five visitors—four of whom are associated with the prison in some official capacity and the fifth a professional from out of state—was subjected to a "pat search" before being let through the first of the three massive locked doors that separate the prison's reception area from its secure units. These searches are routine for prison volunteers and visitors but not for regular prison employees.

The pat searches were thorough. One by one, each of the five visitors was conducted into a small room, ordered to hand over all jewelry except for a wedding or engagement ring and a "small" pair of earrings, and told to remove any clothing such as a jacket or sweater. The clothing was searched; then each visitor had to open her mouth and roll up her tongue to demonstrate that nothing was lodged under it. Next came the actual patting—front, sides, arms, legs and back, impersonal but thorough. Finally each woman stood with her back to the C.O. and stepped out of her shoes, which the C.O. shook vigorously, then presented the soles of her feet for inspection. That ended the search; the visitor's pocketbook and her jewelry were placed in an individual locker, and the key was handed over to a C.O. At last, without being allowed physical or verbal contact with any of the other visitors, each was buzzed through the first door.

In the midst of the talk about searches, the women's group is startled by a thump on the door. "Med line!" a male C.O. shouts. His cry brings everyone but Pamela, Bunny, and Laura to their feet. Off the others go to receive their nightly medication—aspirin and cold remedies for some, insulin for the diabetics, blood pressure pills for those with hypertension, antibiotics for the ones with various types of infections. A few who are depressed may be able to receive antidepressants or tranquilizers, and Sherrie, who is suffering drug withdrawal symptoms, will be given medication to compensate to some degree for the illegal substances her body craves. Pregnant women receive methadone for the same reason, and to protect the health of the babies they carry. C.O.s on the med line will watch each woman closely to make sure she swallows her pills. No one wants stockpiling to fuel a drug party or a suicide attempt.

Prescribing methadone or tranquilizers for prisoners is controversial. Some doctors and penologists frown upon the practice, believing that addicts ought to be forced to quit cold turkey the minute they enter prison. Such deprivation might result in more permanent cures, they suggest.

Others favor medication, and for a variety of reasons. Giving prisoners substitutes for the drugs they are used to keeps them from undergoing the most painful symptoms of withdrawal, they point out. Avoiding withdrawal, in turn, enables them to cope better with the other physical problems from which a majority of them suffer. Another reason advanced for providing medication is that doing so is a vital technique of prison management. Drugging inmates calms them down, keeps them docile and easily disciplined. And discipline, especially in the country's maximum-security institutions, is essential. As a matter of fact, the determination of some prison authorities to keep their facilities under control has led them to drug and tranquilize inmates against their will.

The forced drugging of unwilling prisoners is even more controversial than the practice of offering medication to those who claim to need it. It is irrational, the critics say, to compel addicted prisoners to take calming drugs while at the same time warning them that if they don't stay away from drugs after they are released they will probably find themselves right back in a cell. Among the harshest critics of forced drugging have been prisoners themselves. Some who object to having their feelings and perceptions manipulated on order of prison authorities have taken those authorities to court in an effort to free themselves of unwanted dosages. By the mid-1980s, courts in a few states were beginning to rule in the prisoners' favor.

Many prison officials, however, remain unshaken in their conviction that such rulings are unwise, even dangerous. Drugging is necessary if discipline is to be maintained, they say, because violence is a constant threat in the nation's prisons. They are right about the violence. The April 1986 riot in South Carolina's Kirkland Correctional Institution was no isolated incident. Other prisons that recorded disturbances that year included New York City's Riker's Island facility, the Arizona State Prison Complex at Tucson, and the West Virginia Penitentiary in Moundsville. Early in 1987, rioting broke out in the Pennsylvania State Correctional Institution. In 1971, thirty-three inmates and ten prison staffers perished in a five-day riot and inmate takeover in New York's Attica State Prison.

Even when there is no actual rioting, prison tension may be high. At one New England men's prison with no history of recent trouble, the atmosphere is tense and watchful. Men in their tiered cages look sullenly away as visitors peer through the bars. Those going to classes or recreation rooms move listlessly, yet their bodies never seem to relax. Some lounge in the stairwells or sprawl on the steps, barring passage until a C.O. orders them to move. A few speak to one of the visitors, whom they know as the director of one of the institution's programs, and one or two even smile, but the smiles are small and cold and do not reach their eyes. Anger and hostility glitter there instead.

In many prisons, tensions are more overt. Frequently, they are racial. California and Texas are two states whose prison systems have been afflicted with gangs organized along race lines. In the early 1980s, many Texas prisoners formed white groups, such as the so-called Aryans and the Texas

Mafia, and black ones—the Mandingo Warriors and the Brotherhood Self-Defense Family. Battles flared. Spanish-speaking members of the Mexican Mafia often got into the action as well. From January 1984 to September 1985, fifty-two Texas prisoners died at the hands of other inmates. Besides their fists and feet, the prisoners' weapons included shivs—thin knives—fashioned from parts of metal cots and even from plastic toothbrush handles honed to a deadly point. It may have been of Texas prisoners that Jackson Toby of Rutgers University was thinking when he called inmates the worst feature of American prisons.

In other systems, tensions arise from competition based on work assignments or special privileges. In Maine's State Prison in Thomaston, the trouble has centered on a craft room where prisoners design and produce novelty items to be sold in the prison shop in town. Since the prisoners get to keep what they earn selling their work, and since the size of the prison population means that the craft room cannot accommodate all who wish to use it, arguments abound. In 1980 and again in 1986, the arguments escalated into threats and intimidation. "Novelty kings" emerged, prisoners strong enough and ruthless enough to compel the weaker and more timid to turn over a portion of their profits in exchange for the "privilege" of using the room. Those who refused to pay were brutalized, and one came close to dying when a group tried to force his head into a piece of moving machinery. In both 1980 and 1986, prison authorities clamped down on the trouble-makers, transferring the worst of them to other institutions and barely managing to avoid full-scale rioting.

It's to their credit that they did act against the violence. In some other systems, the authorities have used inmate-against-inmate violence to help them run their facilities. In the late 1970s, for instance, Texas C.O.s and wardens deliberately harnessed such violence and transformed it into a semiofficial tool of discipline. The toughest and most vicious prisoners were formed into an elite corps known as trusties or tenders. According to *Newsweek* magazine, "These inmates had more authority than many guards." They "kept order on their blocks . . . turned their inmates out for work on time and . . . snitched to the . . . [authorities] about inmates who were plotting trouble or filing legal complaints." What did the tenders get for their pains? "Privileges. They wore special clothes. Their cells were never locked. And they carried weapons; [one] kept a four-and-a-half-inch knife in his boot." Bad as Texas prison conditions were under the tenders, they were not unique, and Texas is far from being the only state that has relied upon such a system.

Another source of prison tension is sex. One of the ways in which Americans have traditionally sought to worsen the punishment of prison is by separating convicts from their families and denying them normal sexual contacts. Although some minimum-security prisons have experimented with furlough programs which permit prisoners to make weekend trips home, and a few have allowed conjugal visits between husbands and wives, both visits and furloughs are much less common here than in a number of other countries, especially in Canada and the nations of western Europe. Consequently, homosexuality is widespread in U.S. prisons, although penologists and prison authorities are unable to agree on just how widespread. It is certain, though, that in both men's and women's prisons, the more powerful and demanding prey upon the younger and more submissive, and violence is often the result. C.O.s are quick to report homosexual activity and seek punishment for it, partly because many of them regard such activity as immoral and partly because they know that it frequently leads to jealousy, feuds, and fights.

There is even a hint of homosexuality in this room tonight. As the prisoners return from having taken their medication, "Judy," a sad-faced white woman whose slumped posture and lifeless voice seem to betoken total despair, moves her chair closer to Sissie's. Sissie, perhaps remembering the isolation that will begin for her in a matter of minutes, drapes her arm over Judy's shoulders. "That would never have happened if a C.O. had been in the room," one of the visitors later comments emphatically. "They're absolute death on that."

But was Sissie's gesture a bit of "that"—a homosexual advance? Or was it simple human affection? For there is affection in this room tonight. Despite the fact that this is a prison—a forbidding place of brick and stone, of shadows and echoes, of coercion and deprivation—despite the fact that these women are misdemeanants and felons guilty of robbery, assault, prostitution, and child beating, there is a sense of warmth and caring around the discussion circle. These women are sorry that Sissie faces punishment. Sherrie is troubled by the knowledge that on the other side of the prison fence, hundreds of young girls are starting down her own fifteen-year path of drugs, prostitution, and prison, and she is passionate about her wish to do something to help just one of them. Even with a cigarette in her hand, Bunny was thoughtful enough to suggest separating the smokers and the non-smokers. Bunny is also the one who has made the greatest effort to bring the two Spanish-speakers into the conversation, addressing them from time to time in their own language. And it's Bunny who, at the end of the evening, will come up to each of the visitors in turn, hug her, and whisper, "Thanks for being here. Thanks for helping. I'm going to make it. I really am."

Everyone hopes so. Because prison is, in the end, a terrible place to be, for Bunny or anyone else. The good feelings generated in this discussion tonight are all too uncommon in the nation's penal institutions. Anger, fear, rage, suspicion, terror, and resentment are far more usual, in this prison as in any other.

The evening is almost over, and there's just time for one final question. It comes from the writer. "What's the worst thing about being in prison?"

A pause. Then an angry "Nothing to do!" from Pamela.

"Do this, do that. Orders, orders." This from Sissie.

"A Monday holiday." For once, Sherrie wasn't first with her reply. The medication must be taking effect. "Two days in a row with no mail."

"Loneliness."

"No privacy."

"Knowing you're hooked. Knowing you'll be back."

"My kids live too far away to visit."

"You want to know the worst thing?" Sissie raises her head suddenly and stares straight ahead. "The really worst thing of all? The worst is today." Her voice slows. "It's my birthday, and my mother came to see me. And she said she won't be back. They strip-searched her. She said she won't come again."

No one speaks. Judy looks into her lap. What is she seeing? The desolation of solitary? The open bathroom in the dorm unit? The locks and bars that press in on her every moment of the day and night? What is she hearing? The barked orders? The foul language? The grating, the banging, the clamor? What is she imagining about her future?

Slowly, Judy pushes the words out: "Just being here, that's the worst thing. Just being here."

6

The Problems
With Prisons

U.S. prisons are beset by problems. On that almost everyone would agree. A certain amount of agreement even exists as to what some of those problems are.

Perhaps the first one that comes to mind is overcrowding. As we have seen, state and federal prisoner levels hit record highs in 1986, and officials were predicting that they would continue to rise into the 1990s. They will probably rise beyond that time, too—unless the United States goes to war. One nationally-known penologist points out that the only occasions during which American prison populations have declined have been in wartime. When war comes, he says, "we need our young, poor, undereducated, unskilled and mentally handicapped."

The number of prison cells in this country is rising too, but not as fast as the number of prisoners. According to figures from the Bureau of Justice Statistics, the average amount of living space per inmate declined by 11 percent from 1979 through 1984. Overcrowding was worst in the West, the bureau reported, and growing fastest in the

South, but all over the country, men, women, and children were being stuffed into cramped prison dormitories or sandwiched two or three together into cells barely large enough for one. "There's no such thing as an empty bed in the modern correctional system," a New York prison consultant, Kenneth Ricci, remarked at a 1986 conference in one New England state. His audience nodded knowingly. In their crowded system, troublemakers ordered into solitary confinement were having to wait up to two or three months for a punishment cell to become available. At the same time, the states of Utah and Florida were engaged in the wholesale granting of early parole to reduce overcrowding. Texas was forced to announce a temporary halt in prison admissions early in 1987, after inmate populations there topped the legal ceiling set by a federal court order.

A second problem, as almost everyone would agree, is prison violence. Fights, rapes, stabbings, and beatings are common behind bars. Outbreaks of violence ranging from minor disturbances to full-scale uprisings make news around the country every year. Altogether, in 1984, 131 inmates and 7 C.O.s were listed as homicides.

A third problem perceived by a majority of Americans is that our prisons do not seem to be accomplishing much. Not, at least, if accomplishment is to be measured in terms of prisoner reform, rehabilitation, or correction. Convicted criminals are clapped into cells, kept there for a few months or years, then released—most of them to commit fresh crimes. Research into recidivism rates indicates that half or more of all U.S. prisoners may be repeat offenders.

Why so much recidivism? Why the violence, the overcrowding? Are the three linked in some way? What other problems afflict the nation's prisons? How might they be dealt with? When Americans start looking at questions like these, the agreement breaks down and the arguing begins.

On one level, the debate appears to be between two groups of people with opposite points of view. Those in the first group believe that the basic trouble is that U.S. prison conditions are too soft. American prisoners are pampered and coddled, they charge. Think of all the special privileges and programs they are offered: educational and vocational courses; therapy and self-help sessions; the use of libraries and workout rooms; commissaries that amount practically to supermarkets; conjugal visits and weekend furloughs—even, in a few minimum-security institutions, swimming pools, tennis courts, and golf courses. No wonder prisoners are so willing to become recidivists. What ex-con wouldn't be happy to return to a place that offers all these amenities plus free room and board, free clothing, free personal supplies, and free medical care—even paid jobs? Naturally our prisons are overcrowded, mostly with people who've been in them before. Felons would have to be crazy not to recognize that they're better off in prison than out facing the tough life on the streets.

Not only does the soft life in prison encourage recidivism and thus increase overcrowding; it also undermines prison discipline, these critics maintain. Convicts who can attend school, play games, buy and cook their own food, and work at solving personal problems are hardly suffering the privation and degradation traditionally associated with incarceration. For them, prison is more like a country club than a place of punishment. Yet, pampered as they are, they are not satisfied, and like spoiled children, they demand still more rights and privileges. It's those demands that bring about much of the violence of prison life. How many riots have started over trivial complaints about the quality of prison food? How many because prisoners were denied a special privilege, or because their TV-viewing hours were cut? A lot, or so this group of

99

critics would answer. Violence, recidivism, and overcrowding are linked, they declare, and all stem from one fundamental flaw: American prisons are too lenient.

Not so! responds the other great group of prison critics. These critics do not hesitate to agree that overcrowding, violence, and recidivism are problems. They disagree, however, that those problems have much to do with prison life's being easy.

Anyone who regards prison as comfortable is overlooking its true nature, these critics say. All the "comforts" and "privileges" to be found in the most liberal of institutions pall compared to the horror of incarceration itself. The separation from loved ones, the obstacles placed in the way of thinking or planning for oneself, the loss of individuality and personal identity—these are the real punishments of life in captivity. Television and tennis cannot begin to compensate for them, even when such luxuries are available.

And they're available a lot less than many Americans think, these people add. To have a personal television, for example, a prisoner must first have a personal cell to put it in. In the western states, only a quarter of all inmates are so lucky. Other amenities may be similarly illusory. The "commissary" at many institutions is no more than a couple of vending machines for sodas and snacks. Very few prisons include golf courses, while scores have nonworking showers, toilets that are exposed to public view, or cells in which one inmate sleeps on a cot while one or two others make do with the floor. Work and vocational programs are severely limited as to the number of prisoners they can accommodate, and many inmates who would like to take advantage of them cannot. What is more, privileges often turn into tools for manipulating inmates and bending them to the needs of the institution. Just look at how prisoners were bribed into enforcing the brutal convict-against-convict discipline that dominated the Texas prison system during the late 1970s. Overall, these critics conclude, it's a lack of amenities, not an overabundance of them, that is the problem.

That problem creates others, they go on. Recidivism, for example, they see more as the result of the failure of American prisons to meet their inmates' educational and vocational needs than of the inmates' yearning for the "soft life" of incarceration. It's hardly surprising, they say, that ex-prisoners commit new crimes. Most of them are sent back to the street no better educated or equipped to do honest work than they were when they entered prison. Those who do return to jail or prison contribute to the overcrowding, to be sure, but that is the fault of a system that has done little to help them change their ways. As long as that system remains in place, these critics predict, recidivism will be a problem, and overcrowding will escalate. Violence will escalate along with it, they add, the inevitable result of cooping up hundreds of unhappy human beings together, of jamming three into a space inadequately designed for one, or forty into a room meant for half that number. Like the critics in the first group, these critics see strong links among violence, overcrowding, and recidivism. They just disagree about the nature of those links and the underlying causes of the problems themselves.

Disagreeing about the problems, the two groups naturally disagree about how to go about coping with them. Broadly speaking, those in the second group advocate easing the conditions of prison life, while those in the first would make them harsher.

Former Missouri State Penitentiary inmate J. J. Maloney speaks for the first group. In the 1983 *Saturday Review* article mentioned before, Maloney presents his vision of an effective prison:

In this prison convicts would be given overalls, underwear, socks, and tennis shoes. They would have a flexible toothbrush so it couldn't be sharpened into a weapon, a flexible comb, liquid soap, a towel, and toilet paper. They would be allowed one library book in their cells. No personal property whatever. . . . No one could smoke. . . . Prisoners would spend more time in their cells, as convicts in solitary do now. . . .

At the end of six months, prisoners could enroll in the prison school, which would let them out of their cells four hours a day. . . .

Every moment that a man was out of his cell, he would be under the direct scrutiny of guards . . . the guards would know they had total control.

Maloney recognized the severity of a regimen like this. "A year in such a prison would be like three years in a current prison. Five years would be hard to take. Ten years would be almost too much." And he cautioned that not every present inmate needs or deserves such harsh treatment. "The only people who would need to go to prison would be violent, dangerous offenders: killers, rapists, kidnappers, armed robbers. . . . The only nonviolent crimes that merit a prison term are those in the category of 'criminal enterprise': professional forgery rings, burglary rings, fencing operations, and drug rings."

Strict as Maloney would like to see prisons become, his proposals look mild compared to those put forth by the dean of the School of Criminal Justice at the State University of New York in Albany, a man named Graeme R. Newman. Newman's ideas are radical. "Going to prison should be like reaching a point of no return, like descending into Hell," he wrote in his 1983 book, *Just and Painful: The Case for the Corporal Punishment of Criminals*. Like the English and American Quakers of two hundred years ago, Newman sees a strong religious element in punishment. In order to mend their ways, he believes, criminals must be brought to a state of penitence. Unlike the gentle Friends, however, Newman is convinced that such penitence can be achieved only by "a long process of suffering"—suffering through the application of corporal punishment.

Also unlike the Quakers, Newman can call upon the work of a number of modern scientists to bolster his theories. He cites experiments in which psychologists have used painful electric shocks to "condition" rats, dogs, monkeys, and other animals to avoid food, even when they are hungry. "There is little doubt that, in the experimental conditions of the laboratory, acute pain is a very efficient and lasting suppressor of unwanted behavior," he wrote.

It would be the same outside the lab, and for human beings, Newman contends. Putting "evil people" in prison and subjecting them to powerful electric shocks will bring them to an awareness of the pain and suffering their deeds have caused others. This awareness will enable them to atone for their sins and assume their rightful places as lawful members of society. Even though Newman refers to the behavior-modification experiments of psychology, the electric shocks he recommends would not be justified on the grounds of "treatment," as they were at Maryland's Patuxent Institution in the 1950s and 1960s. They would be retributive punishment, pure and simple.

In Newman's scheme for U.S. prisons, the shocks would be the "preferred corporal punishment" for the "majority of property crimes." In the case of "violent crimes in which the victim was terrified and humiliated," though, ". . . a violent corporal punishment should be considered, such as whipping. In these cases, humiliation of the offender is seen as justifiably deserved." Not only would the punishment bring about

103

the reformation of individual criminals, Newman asserts; the sight of it being inflicted would further serve as a deterrent to the public at large. Another of his suggestions is to make murderers pay for their behavior by forcing them to submit as subjects of "risky" medical research. "It seems morally required that . . . [those who have taken lives] should devote their time to saving lives in whatever way possible, and that they should see it as quite deserving that they should risk their lives for others."

Radical is certainly the word for what Newman proposes. Although prisoners have been used in medical research in the past—it was eighteenth-century English convicts who provided the evidence that smallpox vaccinations were effective, for instance—using them this way is no longer considered ethical. Even allowing prisoners to volunteer for such research was ruled out in the 1970s by a federally created National Commission for the Protection of Human Subjects of Biomedical and Behavioral Research. The commission's reasoning: since prisoners are not physically free, they are incapable of making truly free choices. Any decision a prisoner comes to about whether or not to participate in a research project is bound to contain an element of coercion. Prisoners might volunteer in the belief that doing so will bring them quick parole or new privileges, for instance. And if prisoners are not to be permitted to volunteer to take part in medical research, how can they be forced to do so?

Newman's other ideas seem similarly unlikely to be implemented in U.S. prisons. Whippings are something that most Americans associate with colonial times—or with the barbarities of medieval Europe. Likewise, most Americans would surely be repelled by the calculated cruelty of administering excruciating pain by means of electric shock. Even in states with death-penalty laws, Newman's critics note, the old electric chair is giving way to theoretically more humane injections of lethal drugs.

Many people doubt that the shocks would even be effective in the way Newman claims. A rat's behavior is simply not comparable to a human's, they point out, nor is refusing food in a class with experiencing genuine contrition on a religious plane. Why should pain be supposed to produce penitence anyway? many ask. Wouldn't it be more apt to produce fear and anger, making its victims all the more antisocial and brutal? A final consideration is whether electric shocks would be applied to felons regardless of their health—to thieves and muggers with heart conditions or circulatory problems, for example. If they were, the electric shock might kill them, and thievery and assault might well turn out to be capital crimes once more.

Even the milder suggestions of J. J. Maloney do not seem likely to be put into practice in this country. For two centuries, American penologists and prison reformers have been moving in the direction of better treatment of prisoners and a greater respect for their rights as human beings. The very first prison established in the new United States of America, Philadelphia's Walnut Street Jail, was itself an experiment in humanity. Zebulon Brockway and other reformers of the nineteenth century carried the experiment further, and in this century others have taken up their work. That the country would suddenly abandon two hundred years of effort and revert to the brutal methods of an earlier age appears improbable.

But if prison conditions are not to be made harsher, should they be made easier? Should prisons offer more amenities, particularly those amenities that many Americans believe could be instrumental in reforming criminals and preventing recidivism? Should there be more classes and more job training behind bars? More emphasis on drug rehabilitation and psychiatric counseling? More teachers, chaplains, doctors, and social workers to advise inmates and help them prepare to adjust to the demands of free-world society? The second group of American prison critics urges exactly that.

They seem as unlikely to get their way as Newman and Maloney are to get theirs. There are a couple of reasons why. In the first place, most Americans prefer not to listen to talk about prisons or even to think about them. Prison is an unpleasant topic, and prisoners are generally thought of as unpleasant people. Get criminals off the streets, lock them up, and put them out of mind—that's the idea. "People would rather forget prisons and not deal with them until something like a riot makes them take notice," says Dan Manville, a prison researcher with the American Civil Liberties Union (ACLU). The ACLU is critical of many current prison practices and active in reform movements nationwide.

Another reason that pleas to upgrade prison educational and vocational programs often go unheard has to do with money. Operating a prison is expensive; on average, it was costing $17,324, per year to maintain a single inmate in 1984. In Alaska, the state with the highest per-inmate costs, a whopping $38,587 was going for each prisoner. In 1986 the annual cost per inmate on Rikers Island was reported to be about $43,000.

Almost without exception, Americans deplore the high costs. But they deplore them for very different reasons.

Many resent the amount spent on prisons because of their conviction that the money is going to pay for prisoner luxuries. Law libraries and television lounges, stoves and refrigerators, fancy food and pool tables—that's how they think the taxpayers' prison dollars are spent. Voting to increase prison budgets will only mean more squandered on what has already made America's correctional facilities havens for violent and lazy recidivists, they are sure.

But others disagree, not only about how money for prisons should be spent in the future but about how it has been spent in the past. For the most part, these others say, prisoners themselves pay, directly or indirectly, for any amenities they enjoy. Those who want radios and televisions—and who are permitted to have them—must supply their own or do without. Nor is public money generally expended on sports facilities; where such facilities exist, they are usually paid for with money accumulated out of fees collected from inmates when they make personal telephone calls, use the prison store, or avail themselves of other privileges. Televisions in lounges or recreation rooms are likely to have been purchased with money from similar sources. Prison authorities don't spend overmuch on education or job training, either, these critics go on, which is one reason such programs are so limited.

They don't even spend more than they have to on prisoner necessities. When Attica State Prison erupted into violence in 1971, one prisoner demand was an improved diet—the state was then feeding each inmate for just 72¢ a day. Another was for more toilet paper. The 1971 allotment—one roll for each prisoner every five weeks—was not enough, the prisoners said.

Besides skimping on the basics, prison officials and state and local lawmakers find other ways to save money at inmates' expense. Permitting prisoners to feed themselves from commissaries or to buy and wear their own clothing may sound like coddling—but think how much it saves taxpayers. Prisoners contribute to their own upkeep by performing required housekeeping and custodial tasks as well, and by working in prison shops. Don't forget that the California Prison

Industry Authority had an income of $52 million and saved the state $15 million in just one year. Much of that profit came from the abysmally low wages, 20¢ to 80¢ an hour, paid to inmate workers.

But if public money isn't being wasted on prison frills, where is it going? For security. According to *The Corrections Yearbook,* a maximum-security prison is far more expensive to build than one that affords less protection. In 1984, per-bed construction costs averaged $38,767 for prisons at all security levels. Average construction costs for a maximum-security bed, however, were nearly double that—$75,611. And these figures do not include certain costs, such as interest payments on loans. In the same way, keeping a prisoner under heavy guard is more expensive than keeping that same prisoner in less secure surroundings.

The fact that so much of prison funding goes for security troubles some prison critics. In their view, the emphasis on security throws the entire system out of balance.

Part of the imbalance comes from the fact that re-habilitative programs are routinely sacrificed to what prison officials see as the demands of security. If C.O.s hear a rumor that one prisoner is hoarding contraband, everyone on the cell block may be locked in for hours while a search is made. Hundreds of prisoners lose a day's worth of classes, training, exercise, and therapy. Frequently, the critics charge, the concerns about security are exaggerated. A rumor may be just a rumor, and the learning lost for the sake of contraband that never existed.

Security concerns also add to the bleakness of prison life and to what many see as its "Mickey Mouse" rules—another kind of imbalance, the critics say. Former teacher and girls' school headmistress Jean Harris was convicted in New York in 1981 for the fatal shooting of her estranged lover and was imprisoned there. In a book she wrote while behind bars, Harris tells about the rules regarding the color clothes she and her fellow inmates are allowed to wear. C.O.s at the institution dress in dark blue uniforms and, when needed, orange raincoats. So that prisoners will not be confused with C.O.s, the former are forbidden to wear anything blue, black, or orange. Even the inmates' babies, some of whom are housed in a special nursery at the facility, may not have blue booties on their feet, nor be fed from blue bottles. All, Harris writes indignantly, in the name of security.

The emphasis on security turns prison into a crueler place, too. Female prisoners who are pregnant describe being taken to hospital delivery rooms in handcuffs and leg irons, on the theory that they might otherwise try to escape. Escape at a time like that? In 1986, an inmate of a midwestern county house of correction claimed that she was left to give birth alone in her cell because C.O.s were convinced that she was faking her labor pains, possibly in an escape plot. When she screamed for help, she was threatened with disciplinary action. In 1984 Jean Harris struggled to recover from a life-threatening heart attack while chained to a hospital bed.

Oddly enough, a high level of prison security affords no guarantee that either prisoners or C.O.s will actually be secure. According to the Bureau of Justice Statistics, maximum-security facilities have a higher rate of violence than any other type. Although only a quarter of all prison facilities are classed as maximum security, those facilities experienced over half of all the prison homicides and suicides reported in 1984. That's yet another imbalance.

It is *not,* security-conscious prison authorities snap back. More violence occurs in maximum-security units because it is there that the most violent felons are housed. Furthermore, the officials contend that the situations they face daily provide ample justification for the security measures they take. Drugs and weapons are a reality behind bars, as any prisoner will attest, and both threaten lives as well as prison rules and discipline. Escapes do occur. Precise figures are hard to come by, since reporting methods vary from state to state, but at least 2,594 inmates got away from state and federal prisons in 1984, and another 3,176 walked out while on furlough or participating in work-release programs. Would-be escapees can be unexpectedly creative. One Florida inmate who had spent seven years in a wheelchair fled in 1987 after leaping from the chair, overpowering a C.O., and seizing two hostages. "We had never seen him walk," the astonished prison superintendent told reporters. Given that such daring escapes do occur, it is not difficult to understand that prison officials must be concerned with security.

Still, many Americans persist in their belief that security is overemphasized in U.S. prisons, and that belief adds to the difficulty in increasing prison budgets. Although these Americans would undoubtedly vote more funds for prison education and other programs intended to make it easier for ex-prisoners to succeed on the outside, they do not believe that any additional funding would go for such programs. Any new appropriations, they argue, will only be spent on more of what has already proved so destructive to prisons and their inmates—on more bars and chains and locks, on more bullet-proof glass and fortified command centers, on more C.O.s and guns, on more of what has repeatedly been shown to produce violent prisons full of recidivists who are hurt by the system more than they are helped by it. And so the two great groups of Americans, with their divergent perceptions about prisons and prison ills, and with all their conflicting notions about how to go about curing those ills, stand united on this: In the view of both, substantial increases in prison funding will only perpetuate a bad system and its problems. As a result, the system remains basically unchanged, and violence and recidivism continue.

That leaves the issue of overcrowding. Can't Americans at least agree on how to tackle that problem? Can't we simply build more prisons?

Unfortunately, it's not that easy. For one thing, prison construction is expensive. The thirty-four new state prisons that opened in 1984 cost an average of $10.9 million each to build. Taxpayers are generally reluctant to spend that kind of money, especially for something as unpopular as a prison. Then there is the question of what sort of prisons to build. Minimum security? Those who think American prisons are too soft will vote overwhelmingly against the idea. Maximum security? That will run into opposition from everyone who believes that the emphasis on security itself is a major underlying prison problem.

Another difficulty is that, reluctant as voters are to spend money on prison construction, most are even more reluctant to see that construction getting underway in their own town or city. Prison officials refer wearily to the "nimby" factor in all this. Nimby stands for the almost universal cry: "Not in my backyard." That's the most common reaction when politicians and penologists start proposing a new facility. Put the prison in a remote part of the state, off in the mountains or on the edge of the desert, and isolate murderers and other felons from honest, law-abiding citizens and their families—that's the public attitude. It is an attitude shared equally between those who think prisons are too harsh and those who call them too lenient, and it is an understandable attitude. But it does help create a further problem for corrections officials: When they release prisoners, they are freeing men and women who may have lost the ability to cope with the outside world.

That is because, in most states, voters have gotten their way and prisons have been placed away from major population centers. Prisoners at these institutions are separated, not merely from society at large, but from their own families and friends. This is especially true of the urban blacks who make up so much of the total prison community. Many are confined so far from their homes that family members, who may have low-paying jobs or be on welfare, cannot find the time or money to visit them regularly.

Some Americans see the isolation and the lack of visitors as part of a criminal's punishment, a richly deserved part. Why should a convict, perhaps a murderer who has deprived some other family of a loved one, be permitted to see his own relatives? Is that fair? Maybe not—J. J. Maloney obviously doesn't think it is—but many penologists would argue that it is wise. Only if prisoners can keep their contacts with the outside, they say, do they have much chance of going straight after release. Once freed, former convicts need families to receive them and homes to go to. They also need jobs. Common sense suggests that without all three, a great many ex-cons will be back behind bars in a matter of months. But maintaining a home and family and landing a job are just about impossible for men and women who have been cut off from everyone they know and love for five or ten years or even longer.

Ironically, once a town actually gets a prison, public protests against it usually die down. In 1984, residents of Princess Anne, Maryland, were up in arms over the state's plan to build a correctional facility there. But as the project neared completion two years later, most were delighted. "It's the biggest thing ever to happen," one of the project's former opponents declared. The prison was expected to provide work for as many as 720 people, and in Princess Anne, where unemployment rates were among the state's highest, that was welcome news. "We're talking progress now," said one local politician, as job-hungry families began moving to the town and building homes. Huntsville, Texas, is another town that depends for its livelihood upon its prison. The Texas Department of Corrections, headquartered in Huntsville, employs 4,500. In many Huntsville families, prison jobs are handed down from one generation to the next. By the mid-1980s, civic boosters there were developing plans to lure tourists to town by setting up a prison museum. The centerpiece for the new attraction was to be "Old Sparky," the electric chair used in Texas executions from 1924 to 1964.

If the people of Huntsville and Princess Anne can look so favorably upon the prisons in their midst, can't people in other places be convinced that they, too, will benefit from becoming home to a population of convicts? It is possible, but even if they do, even if Americans start welcoming new prisons and cheering their construction, it would have little impact on prison overcrowding. That is because, as things are now, no matter how many prisons this country erects, there will never be enough.

"You can't build your way out of this," one New York penologist warned in 1986. "The more you build, the more they fill up." To understand why, Americans do not have to look much beyond the mandatory sentencing laws they have urged upon federal, state, and local legislators in recent years. We saw in Chapter 4 the effect that such laws have had on Washington, D.C., jails.

Also ensuring continued overcrowding is the current movement toward abolishing parole on the state and federal levels. A third factor is that there are already thousands of convicted felons and misdemeanants out wandering the streets because there is no room for them in prison. There are also thousands of men and women released—prematurely, some say—from hospitals and other facilities for the mentally ill or disturbed. Such people may be unequipped to deal with society, and as a consequence, they often run afoul of the law. Homeless people, Americans who have lost their jobs or their farms, may get into trouble, too. We could spend years building prisons to hold all these people and still not have space for them all. As if that weren't enough, it is a fact well known to penologists that empty cells act as virtual magnets to attract new prisoners. As long as the public knows that the cells are there, people will demand longer and longer sentences for criminals. Prosecutors will urge judges to impose maximum terms, and judges will comply. Almost as soon as it is built, each new cell will be filled with one . . . two . . . three new inmates. That is what Kenneth Ricci meant when he told his New England audience that there's no such thing as an empty bed in U.S. corrections systems.

Where does all this leave us? With some pretty stubborn-looking problems. Prisons seem set to remain overcrowded, no matter what we do about building more. Violence and recidivism will continue as long as Americans go on simultaneously ignoring their prisons and disagreeing over how they ought to be run. We end up, it seems, with the same three problems with which we began, and that, to many Americans, suggests that the whole system needs to be overhauled. Perhaps, some say, it's time for governments to start removing themselves from the prison business.

One way to accomplish that is for governments to contract out for certain prison services. Private caterers or food suppliers can be hired to provide inmate meals, for example. Classroom and vocational programs can be taken out of the control of prison administrators and placed in the charge of professional educators. Medical services can be farmed out to private doctors or health-care groups. Getting health care into the hands of competent outside professionals would be a particularly good move, say many who are familiar with prison conditions. As of 1986, about a third of the nation's city and county jails were involved in legal suits brought by prisoners and their advocates and charging dangerously substandard medical care. At the same time, more than half of all state corrections departments were under court order to upgrade their medical facilities.

The demands on prison health care will be even greater in the future, most believe, as the disease AIDS—acquired immune deficiency syndrome—continues to spread. So far, this invariably fatal disease has been most common among two groups: men who engage in homosexual activities and drug addicts who share needles infected with the AIDS virus. Both groups are well represented in U.S. prisons, and prison officials are bracing for a devastating AIDS epidemic. If and when it comes, it will be essential to have the best and most efficient medical services available. The only alternative will be to release AIDS prisoners early on a sort of "compassionate parole"—as officials in some states have already started to do.

Even now, a number of states are contracting out for various prison services. California and Washington spend the most on contracting. Next comes the Massachusetts juvenile system and the federal system, followed by Illinois, Florida, Maryland, and Michigan. Services most frequently provided by private companies involve health, education, drug treatment, construction, halfway houses, vocational training, and religion.

And that may be only the start for the private sector in American prisons. If companies like Corrections Corporation of America (CCA), of Nashville, Tennessee, have their way, all the country's jails and prisons will one day be turned over to private enterprise.

CCA was founded in 1983, and within two years the company was operating four prisons, one each in Texas and North Carolina and two in Tennessee. One of the Tennessee institutions was a juvenile facility; the other, a multipurpose institution for adults. The company's North Carolina prison holds federal prisoners, and its Texas center houses a population of the country's fast-growing number of illegal aliens.

Private prisons are nothing new. Many of the earliest English jails were privately owned and managed, and it was private shipowners who signed contracts to transport English felons to penal colonies such as those established in Australia after 1787. Private prisons are the wave of the future, too, people like CCA vice-president Travis Snellings are convinced. "Our basic mission is to provide correctional services to government in an efficient, cost-effective manner," he says.

Snellings' conviction that CCA and other similar companies can fulfill that mission has several bases. One is that private companies can run their operations out of the public eye and insulated from public pressures. Their policies cannot be scrutinized and questioned the way government operations can be. Nor are those policies likely to be affected by political maneuvering on the part of ambitious office seekers or elected and appointed officials. Finally, advocates of the private system point out, they can hire staff members on the basis of ability and competence, not because of their political connections. Political patronage, which has often played a role in the selection of prison officials, has contributed to inefficiency and poor management at all levels, they say.

Private prisons would also be more effective than government-run ones, the private companies promise. Ted Nissen, head of Behavior Systems Southwest, which operates both federal and local facilities, brings up the problem of recidivism in public prisons. "We have a national recidivism rate of fifty percent," he complains. "I offer to forfeit my contracts if the recidivism rate is more than forty percent."

Last but not least, a private system will be less costly for the taxpayer than the present public system, its proponents claim. In 1985, for instance, the federal government was paying CCA $23.84 a day for each inmate confined in its Texas center for illegal aliens. Illegal aliens in its own facilities were costing the government nearly $3.00 a day more, $26.45 for each twenty-four hours of detention. Part of the CCA saving came in C.O.s salaries; private companies can set their own pay levels, while governments may have to match higher state or federal civil service standards. The saving also owed something to the speed with which the owners and managers of a private concern can make decisions and carry them out. They have no need to wait for months while lawmakers wrangle about funding levels and prices soar. Private prisons have shown themselves to be cost-effective so far, people like Nissen and Snelling say, and they will continue to do so. Cost-effectiveness is what companies like CCA and Behavior Systems Southwest are all about, after all. They are in business to make a profit.

That is exactly what some Americans find so disturbing about them, and about the entire idea of private prisons. Is it right, they ask, for someone to be profiting from the incarceration and punishment of others? It is upsetting enough, many say, that towns like Huntsville, Texas, and Princess Anne, Maryland, live off their prisoners and even seek to exploit them through a museum display of grisly prison artifacts. It is bad enough that prison industries and the states that run them benefit so handsomely from the near-slave wages they offer their workers. But to run prisons in order to make a *profit* is something else again. Companies like CCA are corporations with stockholders who have invested their own money and who expect to see a return on it. Profits—not reform, correction, rehabilitation, or even punishment—that's what private prisons are all about.

How can the profit motive help affecting the inmates? "I've got to think like Colonel Sanders," Ted Nissen says. "I'll try anything. If it works and I make a profit, I'll stick with it." The shippers who conveyed English prisoners to Australia in the nineteenth century had the same attitude. They were in business to make a profit, too, and they did so by charging the government per convict head, then loading as many aboard as their ships would take. Once at sea, the prisoners were locked in filthy holds and fed at starvation levels. Sometimes half of them died before reaching land.

Modern American prisoners are just as likely to be abused if this country shifts to a system of private prisons, many people warn. The very fact that CCA and other private companies are shielded from public scrutiny means that the abuses will be given every opportunity to go unnoticed and uncorrected. Critics of the private system note that although government officials are supposed to inspect private prison facilities and monitor their operations, the inspections are lax or spotty. It will become even spottier as private prisons increase in number, they fear.

Others have different concerns about for-profit incarceration. Up to this point, the country's private institutions have suffered many of the same kinds of problems that prevail in public facilities. Among other incidents, a juvenile committed suicide at a private youth detention center in Pennsylvania and a CCA guard shot and killed one alien and wounded another at its Texas center. In a second private institution in Texas, a depressed woman begged guards for six weeks to be allowed to talk with a psychiatrist. Eventually, she slipped into a catatonic state and had to be hospitalized. Why had she been kept from consulting a doctor? Because the prison's budget, prepared with an eye to profits, did not allow for a psychiatrist on staff. By contrast, troubled prisoners at federally run institutions are routinely seen by psychiatrists of the U.S. Public Health Service.

Some also wonder if private prisons will turn out to be as effective as their admirers say they will. Is a recidivism rate of 40 percent really a great improvement over a rate of 50 percent? Cost-effectiveness could be an unattainable goal, too, even with corner cutting in such areas as psychiatric care. In 1986, a private facility in Pennsylvania went broke, listing debts of $719,000 compared with assets of only $384,000. The day after prison officials filed for bankruptcy, the Pennsylvania legislature passed a bill banning any new private correctional institutions pending an examination of their performances to date, particularly with regard to the rights of prisoners.

Do private prisons represent the way of the future? Travis Snelling and Ted Nissen are sure of it. Despite the doubts and the drawbacks, they maintain, American penology must be put in private hands. The public systems are simply not working, and governments must abandon them.

What about governments in other countries? some Americans ask. Have they done better than we have at managing their prisons? Can we learn a lesson from them?

The answer to that is yes—and no. The prison systems of nations like the Soviet Union, South Africa, and many of the countries of South and Central America are notorious, of course. Part of the reason for that is that prison populations there include hefty percentages of men, women, and even children who are detained, not because they have committed any crime, but because of their political opposition to the government. For them, the conditions of confinement are apt to be brutal, and physical and mental torture a daily reality. In addition, Soviet political prisoners are commonly subjected to abusive psychiatric "treatment."

In a number of other nations, though, conditions are much less harsh. In Canada and much of Western Europe, a great deal of emphasis is placed on helping prisoners prepare to readjust to life in the outside world. The Correctional Service of Canada (CSC), for instance, encourages inmates to keep up their family ties, and extensive furloughs and frequent conjugal visits are the rule. Canada also tries to use prisons to instill good work habits. Pay for those in prison industries ranges from $3.15 to $7.55 per day.

Still, prisons in Canada and Western Europe do suffer from many of the same problems common in U.S. institutions. They, too, may be overcrowded. With a capacity of 11,068 inmates, the CSC was housing 12,405 in 1984. The next year, England, with room for only 40,300, had nearly 50,000 behind bars. Elsewhere, crowding is not a problem. Sweden, with room for 4,175, had just 3,260 prisoners in the mid-1980s. Norway, with room for 2,250 in its prisons, was holding 1,873. What's more, prisons in the Scandinavian countries are designed to be small institutions. Many hold no more than 100 or 200 inmates. Sentences are short compared to sentences in the United States. Shorter sentences and the lack of crowding helps cut down on violence, compared to American institutions. Violence is a problem in England and Canada, though. British institutions saw serious riots in the mid-80s. Thirty Canadian inmates and two guards died violent deaths in 1984. Recidivism is a problem in Canada as well—41.5 percent as of 1984.

The fact that Canada's prison problems so closely reflect

those of the United States—although they exist on a smaller scale—must be discouraging to American prison officials. In its size and ethnic complexity, Canada is much more like this country than are the Scandinavian nations. If the Canadian government is not much better at solving its problems than the U.S. government, it does not provide much of a model for prison officials here.

And that suggests, once again, that it really may be time for government to get out of the prison business. Even some of the severest critics of the idea of private prisons agree with that. Government has failed to manage its penal systems and should abandon the effort, they say. But that does not mean prisons should be turned over to private enterprise. Instead, governments ought to abolish their prisons altogether.

7

Community Corrections

Dr. Jerome Miller didn't set out to shut down the Massachusetts juvenile prison system when he took over as commissioner of that state's Department of Youth Services in 1969. It just happened that way. All Miller really meant to accomplish were a few reforms.

Back in the late 1960s, the 123-year-old system stood in need of some changing. Descended from the first public reform school established for boys in the United States, the Massachusetts system consisted of four prison facilities holding about a thousand "delinquent" boys and girls. In addition, three state training schools served to house "habitual truants and school offenders." Each of the youngsters in the system had run into trouble with the law at an early age, and many were already hardened criminals. The majority came from so-called disadvantaged backgrounds: 90 percent from families on welfare and 60 percent from families with a history of drug or alcohol problems, mental instability, and child abuse.

By most accounts, the training schools and prisons in which these young lawbreakers found themselves were brutal places. Staffed under the political patronage system, guards and administrators were, in Miller's words, people "whose talents lay more in running political campaigns than in rehabilitating youthful offenders." Untrained and unprofessional as they were, however, the guards enjoyed wide discretion in deciding on punishments and handing them out. Harassment was routine, and beatings, restricted diets, and solitary confinement were the penalties for even relatively minor rule breaking. The infractions did not have to be deliberate; children were disciplined for bed-wetting, among other things. At one training school, serious misbehavior warranted a spell alone in the "tombs"—a series of unlighted cells, each measuring six feet by three feet.

As tends to be the way with prisons, the brutality did not come cheap. By the early 1970s, it was costing Massachusetts $10,000 a year to maintain a single juvenile inmate. (Fifteen years later, the national average per-prisoner cost of a year in reform school had soared to $30,000.) "For this money," Massachusetts Governor Francis Sargent said of the 1970 figure, "we could buy each child a complete wardrobe at Brooks Brothers, give him a $20 a week allowance, send him to a private school and, in the summer, send him to Europe with all expenses paid. We could do all that and still save the taxpayer over $1300 a year."

It was Sargent who appointed Miller, a social worker by profession, to his post. Throughout 1969 and 1970, the new commissioner, with Sargent's strong backing, struggled to improve conditions in the system. It was a futile struggle. "I said we won't use isolation any more," Miller later recalled. "We won't shave the kids' heads. We'll get trained staff in there, make them more therapeutic. And even in my own system, having made those changes, having sent out those directives, I could never be sure that at 10 o'clock on a given night Johnny

Smith wasn't being wiped off a wall." And so, on January 3, 1971, Miller closed one training school, and within a year, the rest of the state's juvenile prisonlike institutions were things of the past as well. Their abolition was, in the admiring words of one penologist, "without precedent in any penal system in the world."

For most of the youngsters who had been in the system before that January 3, the changes were swift and welcome. Many were sent to halfway houses around the state, while others were parceled out to group homes or individual foster homes. If one arrangement did not seem to be working out, another was tried, and if that proved unsatisfactory, a third and a fourth. Children could be moved from one foster family to another or from one setting to another. The flexibility meant that troubled boys and girls had more of a chance than ever before of ending up in a situation in which each felt comfortable and could do well. "That's the main result of what Miller did," comments a Massachusetts professor who has spent her life working and teaching in the field of corrections. "There's a much greater variety of places available for kids today."

Yet the penologist clearly has reservations about Miller's dramatic experiment. She is quick to point out that the new system is not saving the state as much money as some had hoped it would. It is no less expensive to support a juvenile under the new system than it was under the old. There is, however, a difference in the way the money is being spent. Under the reform school system, 95 percent of the Massachusetts juvenile corrections budget went for institutional upkeep—chiefly staff salaries—and only 5 percent on programs designed to integrate truants, troublemakers, and delinquents back into society. With Miller's system in place, those proportions have been reversed. What is more, Miller's backers remind their critics, if the new system works, it will save money in the long run, because new juvenile prisons will not need to be built or old ones renovated.

Miller's critics also complain that the new system has done little to deter young criminals. The juvenile crime rate remained constant in the Bay State throughout the changes. "There are just as many kids in trouble now as there used to be," the Massachusetts professor remarked in 1986. True, but according to statistics collected by Michael A. Kroll, a former director of the National Moratorium on Prison Construction (NMPC), Massachusetts juvenile offenders are less likely than they once were to grow up to become adult criminals. In 1969, Kroll says, close to 50 percent of the state's adult prisoners had been imprisoned as children as well. By the early 1980s, under 20 percent had passed through the juvenile system.

After leaving his Massachusetts post, Jerome Miller moved to Washington, D.C., to head the National Center on Institutions and Alternatives (NCIA). There he deliberately seeks to accomplish on a nationwide basis what he achieved almost by accident in Massachusetts—a shift from a prison-based correctional system to one that has its roots in the community. Sending as many convicted criminals as possible to prison for as long as possible will always be the most expensive and least effective way of dealing with them, Miller and others like him contend. As much as 80 or 90 percent of the present inmate population could be allowed into the community, they say, and supervised there without danger to the public. It is the goal of groups like NCIA and NMPC to convince a majority of Americans that they are right.

It will take some convincing. Our prisons are riddled with problems, such as overcrowding and violence, and Americans know it. Our prisons are not working; hardly a convict in this country has ever been reformed, rehabilitated, corrected, or brought to penitence by being in prison. When a prisoner does manage to straighten out and avoid recidivism, it's as likely to be in spite of the system as because of it. Americans are aware of that, too. Yet despite all that they know about prison failures and prison problems, people in this country maintain a tenacious faith in the idea of prisons as places of punishment. The thought of abolishing them is just about inconceivable to most Americans. Even the notion that prisons have not always been around, and that they are a relatively recent substitute for more barbarous forms of punishment, is foreign to most Americans. Most would probably react with disbelief at hearing such a thing.

Nevertheless, it is true. Imprisonment as a punishment in and of itself is only about two hundred years old. Prisons are not inevitable in human society. They can be shut down and abandoned, as they were in Massachusetts when Jerome Miller transformed the state's juvenile system in 1971. The system of community corrections that Miller put in place of the prisons has not solved all of Massachusetts' juvenile-justice problems. Still, it does appear to have succeeded in cutting recidivism and in deflecting at least some young culprits from their criminal ways. Surely that is a worthwhile accomplishment, one that could be repeated in other places with other prisoners.

It is important to note that alternatives to strict and conventional imprisonment do not necessarily mean tossing criminals out onto the streets. Some community-involvement programs, in fact, are based upon continued incarceration. An example of such a program is the work-release system run through the Lincoln County Jail in the state of Maine.

Every weekday morning, a number of prisoners at that facility are let out to travel to nearby jobs. Late in 1986, one woman was commuting to the business she herself had founded and owned, for example, while several men were working at the high-paying shipyard jobs they had held before their arrests and convictions. Jail administrator Sergeant Gerald Silva swears by the work-release system and thinks it makes sense. If being in jail causes workers to lose their means of livelihood, he says, they will only be more of a burden to society when they finally are released. At his jail, working inmates pay for the box lunches the cook puts up for them each day, and they also pay rent on their cells. The money makes up for the extra expenses of work-release programs—added work hours for staff who must search inmates for contraband each time they reenter the facility, for instance. The fact that work-release prisoners pay their own way also helps them learn a sense of responsibility, Sergeant Silva believes. If programs like this one were made available to more prisoners, more ex-cons would emerge from prison equipped to be responsible, productive members of society, groups like NCIA and NMPC assert.

Furloughs and conjugal and family visiting are other alternatives to traditional confinement. As Canadian prison officials have found, all three allow convicted criminals to maintain the family contacts that they will find essential when they are freed and must try to readjust to life outside the prison walls. Family visits, which commonly involve the children of convicts, are especially valuable, many believe. Besides keeping adult prisoners actively interested in their offspring and concerned about their well-being, they may also lessen the chances that criminal behavior will be passed on to the next generation. Children from families that remain close despite the imprisonment of a parent are less likely to run into trouble with the law than those whose families break apart completely.

Another alternative to incarceration in a conventional prison could be a stay in a rigorous facility designed along the lines of a U.S. Marine Corps boot camp. Some southern states, including Georgia, Florida and Mississippi, have begun experimenting with such "shock incarceration" camps for young offenders, and by late 1986, New York City officials were considering following their lead. Kevin Frawley, the city's criminal-justice coordinator, described the sort of facility he had in mind. "Not something oppressive," he explained, "just a regimen that would deter further criminal conduct." Keeping such a camp from becoming too oppressive could be a problem, of course. We've seen throughout this book how often well-meant programs of prison reform degenerate into new tools and weapons for punishing prisoners and degrading them. Marine Corps boot camps are themselves tough places—injuries and even deaths do occur among recruits. Conditions would undoubtedly be far tougher for young delinquents and criminals living and working under the supervision of prison guards, and prison camps for young offenders might well turn out to be as cruel and brutal as many present-day facilities.

It is precisely because of considerations such as this one that organizations like NCIA and NMPC advocate the abolition of prisons rather than their reform. Reform efforts have failed or fallen short over and over in the past, the groups contend, and it is hopeless to persist in them. It is time for this country to forget about prisons and turn wholeheartedly to a system of corrections based in the community.

The country has already begun a few small experiments in community corrections. In Massachusetts, Miller turned to group homes and halfway houses to hold young offenders. Similar homes and houses can be used for adults. At the Alston Wilkes Home in Columbia, South Carolina, for instance, forty men and women live together in a setting that bears no resemblance to an ordinary prison. The home's residents range in age from a man of close to seventy who spent three decades in prison on a rape conviction to a seventeen-year-old deemed too old for a juvenile detention center yet not old enough for a regular adult facility. They share kitchen and grounds-keeping duties, observe a 10 P.M. curfew, and are required to forsake alcohol and other drugs. Those at the Alston Wilkes Home live under the supervision of a woman who has been directing such homes since 1983 and receive counseling from professionals and specially trained volunteers. Everyone there has, or is looking for, a job.

Community service is another nonprison alternative presently being offered to some convicts, particularly to those found guilty of white-collar crimes. We've already seen that doctor-convicts may be sentenced to provide low-cost health care, lawyer-convicts to advise the needy in legal matters, and so on. Similar substitutions—service instead of prison—should be made in the case of other types of criminals, many believe. Cleanup tasks in national parks and forests, repair work on the nation's aging roads and bridges, and contributions to environmental land and water reclamation projects are among the public service possibilities. Advocates of such programs emphasize that not only would they be a way for criminals to repay their debts to society; they would also provide more in the way of meaningful job training than many of the vocational classes currently being offered behind bars. Like group homes and halfway houses, community service is a nonprison alternative that judges should use far more often than they do, Miller and others say.

Other types of alternative sentences are only beginning to come into use around the country. In the 1980s, the state of Georgia became a leader in something called intensive probation. More formally known as an Intensive Supervision Program (ISP), this type of punishment allows criminals who would normally be sentenced to terms in prison to remain at home and keep their jobs. But they do both under a surveillance so close that it amounts to virtual house arrest.

It is the closeness of the surveillance that distinguishes intensive probation from regular probation. Whereas an ordinary probationer may have to check in with a probation officer only once every week or month, anyone on ISP must check in five times a week. And while a regular probation officer may be keeping tabs on as many as 100 or 150 people at a time, each team of two ISP officers is responsible for a mere 25 cases. Furthermore, men and women on ISP are regarded as prisoners, not as probationers. Even though they live at home, they are no more free than a prisoner in a work-release program. Except with special permission, ISP prisoners are allowed only in their homes or at work. No bars. No movies. No shopping malls. Nothing—except with specific permission from the ISP team. Their homes and persons are subject to search at any time and without notice. So strict are ISP conditions in Georgia, one penologist reports, that "some . . . people have elected to go back to jail. It's easier."

ISPs can do a great deal to help solve America's prison problems, their proponents believe. Obviously, they could help to relieve overcrowding. A second advantage should be financial. Unlike some other forms of community corrections, ISPs really do save money. The yearly cost of intensive probation runs at about $2,500, a fraction of the average of over $17,000 a year the country was spending per prisoner in the mid-1980s. "You can save the taxpayers an awful lot of money," says Peter J. Tilton, named to head intensive probation in Maine when that state instituted an ISP of its own in 1986. "You can turn a tax liability into a tax asset with the person working and paying taxes while he doesn't have to be supported" in a state prison. Compared to regular probation, though, the intensive supervision is expensive. Regular probation costs average $810 per individual each year.

Naturally, there are those with objections to ISPs. Some think the programs are too easy on criminals. Others fear that judges will hand out ISP sentences to men and women who would otherwise have been put on regular probation or given fines or suspended sentences. If that happens, ISPs will do nothing to relieve prison overcrowding. Most serious of all is the concern about public safety. If murderers and rapists are put into ISPs, the citizenry could be in danger. Maine's Peter Tilton has an answer to that fear. "We're not going to let anyone in the program who's really violent. . . ," he says. "No one convicted of rape or sexual assault will be eligible and no one who has escaped or been convicted of aiding or abetting escape."

ISPs could be made even more rigorous by the introduction of a computerized radio device that some have dubbed an "electronic ball and chain." This ball and chain consists of a lightweight radio transmitter that is strapped to a prisoner's ankle and left there twenty-four hours a day. The radio is linked, through the prisoner's home telephone, to a central computer that registers every one of his or her comings and goings. "For example, when he leaves to go to work, the computer printout says 'LEFT HOME 8 AM VALID,'" a Nassau County, New York, probation department spokesperson explained. Nassau County was one place where the electronic device was being tried out in 1986. West Palm Beach, Florida, was another.

When the ISP prisoner violates probation conditions, that information, too, is reported. "LEFT HOME VIOLATION" appeared on the Nassau County computer printout in relation to one prisoner twice in a single month. On both occasions, the transmitter revealed that the prisoner had paid an unauthorized early-morning visit to his girlfriend's house. If convicted of the violation, this prisoner could be sent to jail for ninety days—the intensive probation time to which he was originally sentenced.

Still other alternative sentences hark back to one of the most ancient of all forms of criminal justice—restitution. Under a Florida program, young, nonviolent thieves and robbers may be required to pay their victims back by working for them without pay until the loss has been made good. In Minnesota, a county judge came up with an unusual restitution-type sentence for a teenager who, in a rage at his girlfriend, snapped the radio antennas off a row of parked cars. Forty-five days in jail, the judge said, the sentence to be lifted immediately if the young man would track down his victims, apologize to each, and pay for a new antenna. It was not an easy task to accomplish while languishing in a jail cell, but the boy rose to the challenge. He took an ad in the local paper asking his victims to get in touch with him, and they did. The apologies followed, and long before the forty-five-day sentence would have been up, restitution was being made.

Other judges have experimented with sentencing offenders to medical treatment rather than prison. Men and women convicted on drunk driving offenses, for instance, may be offered a choice between going to prison and submitting to regular doses of Antabuse, a chemical that reacts with alcohol, causing dizziness and violent nausea. So effective is Antabuse that no one would be able to take it, drink, and still drive. Like other nonprison alternatives, the administration of Antabuse has the advantage of permitting a convict to remain self-supporting and taxpaying. A number of medical experts, though, are critical of Antabuse sentencing. The drug may keep someone from being a highway menace, they say, but it does nothing to cure the underlying problem: the disease of alcoholism. Doctors also warn that Antabuse can produce dangerous side effects in some patients.

Judges have ordered medical treatments for other types of offenders as well, particularly for those found guilty of sex crimes. In 1983, a South Carolina judge sentenced three young rapists to a choice between thirty years in prison and castration by a surgeon. In other states, imprisoned sex offenders have been freed after undergoing chemical castration. Chemical castration is achieved with regular doses of a female hormone called Depo-provera. Depo-provera, like Antabuse, has come under fire from those who warn of such possible side effects as allergic reactions and blood clots, and its popularity among judges has diminished since the 1970s. Surgical castration, too, has its critics. In 1985, the South Carolina Supreme Court ruled that the prison-or-castration sentences handed down to the three rapists were unconstitutional. The sentences violated the Eighth Amendment to the Constitution, the court said, and it ordered the rapists to begin serving their thirty-year terms.

Yet some forms of medical or psychiatric treatment continue to intrigue judges eager to come up with alternatives to incarceration. One New England judge has developed a plan to encourage sex abusers of children to identify themselves by promising help for those who do—and penalizing those who do not. The help would come in the form of private, discreet psychological counseling. The penalty for those who did not come forward—and who got caught—would be a publicized trial and even harsher prison sentences than would generally be imposed.

Other judges concentrate on trying to devise punishments to fit each particular crime. In West Deptford, New Jersey, municipal court judge David Keyko sentences chronic drunk drivers to visit the scenes of fatal crashes caused by too much alcohol. He seeks, as he puts it, "to provide a more graphic visualization of the possible consequences" of operating under the influence. But that visualization is only part of the kind of sentence Judge Keyko started handing out in 1986. The driver must also accompany the police delegation that breaks the tragic news to the victim's family. In addition, he or she pays a fine, undergoes alcoholic rehabilitation therapy, forfeits his or her driver's license for ten years, and performs three months of community service. In Detroit, Michigan, district court judge Leon Jenkins sentences some of the young people who come before him to *school.* Instead of giving one young traffic violator and school dropout a $500 fine or a few weeks in jail, Jenkins ordered him to earn a General Educational Development certificate. The GED certificate is the equivalent of a high school diploma. The boy started studying, got his GED, and within two years was a sophomore in a Detroit college.

Can such innovative sentences really turn young criminals around? Can programs like intensive parole and supervised group living for more serious offenders accomplish all that groups like NCIA and NMPC claim? Will they allow us to empty our prisons, ending overcrowding and saving millions in prison construction and operating costs? Will they, because they permit convicts to keep their old jobs or to train for new ones, break the dismal pattern of recidivism? Might they, by keeping criminals in touch with their families—and with the community—ease the transition from a lawless life to an honest one? Might they reduce the unrealistic expectations that Americans have long held onto for their prisons?

Some are positive they can. They are sure, as well, that Americans will eventually come to see that, and to accept the idea that community corrections and nonprison alternatives can do more to promote justice and reduce crime than imprisonment ever has. After all, they remind us, people have changed their ideas about incarceration and imprisonment in the past. We used to lock our poor in the poorhouse, our homeless and orphaned in the workhouse, our mentally ill in the madhouse. Over the years, we have learned to substitute hospitals, welfare programs, job training, foster homes, and all the rest for locking up the poor, the ill, and the homeless. Perhaps one day we will look back on the late twentieth century as the time when Americans began finding better ways than prison of coping with their criminal populations.

Those who seek to change our minds about the country's dependence upon prisons also remind us that this would not be the first time Americans have changed their thinking about crime and punishment. Three hundred years ago, "witches" were being executed in Massachusetts, and brandings, whippings, and other forms of corporal punishment were inflicted throughout the colonies. We in this country made one great change in our thinking back in 1790, when the first penitentiary was established. We made others when we changed our laws to permit probation and parole, youth reformatories, separate institutions for female convicts, and such facilities as halfway houses and prerelease centers. Can we not change our attitudes again—recognize that imprisonment was an experiment that is not working—and try something new?

Perhaps—and perhaps not. For the idea that prison must follow conviction is deeply etched in American minds. Jerome Miller learned that when he began shutting down the juvenile prisons in Massachusetts. The public protested loudly, and so did the police, judges, probation officers, and prison officials. Without Governor Sargent firmly behind him, the pressure would have forced Miller to give up his efforts.

"The sad truth," says Judge Terry Smerling of the Los Angeles municipal court, "is that Americans have a mania for incarceration exceeded in the industrialized world only by the Soviet Union and South Africa." Judge Smerling made this observation in a column that appeared in *The Los Angeles Times* in September 1986. In the column, the judge argued in favor of the kind of creative alternative sentencing examined in this chapter. "Our obliviousness to the extravagance and ineffectualness of incarceration deprives our criminal justice system of the ingenuity and progress that we rightfully should expect," the column concluded.

Judge Smerling is not the only judge who feels this way. In 1972, a Wisconsin judge, James Doyle, expressed himself even more forcefully. "I am persuaded," Doyle wrote, "that the institution of prison probably must end. In many respects it is as intolerable within the United States as was the institution of slavery, equally brutalizing to all involved, equally toxic to the social system, equally subversive of the brotherhood of man, even more costly by some standards, and probably less rational."

Yet not even Judge Doyle or Judge Smerling—not even Jerome Miller—would demand the total abolition of all jails and prisons. Even if prosecutors and judges used alternative sentencing and community corrections to the maximum extent possible, some men and women, and some children, too, would be left behind bars. Remember that although many wardens and other prison professionals contend that 80 or 90 percent of all U.S. prisoners could safely be released, that leaves 10 or 20 percent who could not. Even after closing the Massachusetts juvenile system, Dr. Miller found himself with forty or fifty youngsters who, for one reason or another, seemed simply incapable of adjusting to any kind of community setting. They required intensive supervision and psychological care. To receive both, they were housed in the state's only two remaining juvenile prison facilities.

So it would be with the overall prison population. Even if America does turn to community corrections and begins to tear its prisons down, some prisoners will remain among us. And so we must still ask the questions: What should our prisons be like? How should our prisoners be treated?

8

Prisoners as Human Beings

How should prisoners be treated? That question has been asked, and answered—in several different ways—during the past two hundred years.

The first time the question came up in the young United States, the Quakers of Philadelphia offered a prompt response: prisoners should be treated with kindness. It was kindness and a sincere desire to see criminals repent and become good citizens that led these reformers to convert the jail on Walnut Street into a model penitentiary.

But attitudes of kindness toward prisoners did not run deep in the United States even then. Beyond the reformers lay the vast American public, a public outraged by the crimes committed against it and determined to punish wrongdoers swiftly and harshly. From this public came the prison C.O.s and wardens, the judges and juries, the prosecutors and police, and all the others whose job it was to deal with suspects and convicts on a daily basis. They, and not the reformers, were the men and women who shaped and molded our prison systems.

It did not take long for those systems to become permeated with the anger and vindictiveness of the people running them. Kindness and the idea of inducing penitence were quickly swallowed up in the brutalities of the silent and solitary theories of punishment. Other reforms were introduced over the years, but they, too, were touched and warped by vengeful attitudes. Men, women, and children were locked up in the nation's prisons and told they were there to be "reformed," "rehabilitated," "trained," "corrected," or "treated." But the prisoners themselves knew better. They could see precious few genuine efforts at reform, rehabilitation, training, correction, or treatment, and their position was plain to them. They were not in prison to be helped; they were there so that society could avenge itself upon them. And there was nothing they could do about it. They were at the mercy of their captors. As prisoners, they had no rights at all.

American prisoners' lack of rights was spelled out flatly by the U.S. Supreme Court in 1871. Ruling against a man who had brought suit against prison authorities for violating his constitutional rights, the justices found: "He [the prisoner] has as a consequence of his crime, not only forfeited his liberty, but all his personal rights. . . . He is for the time being the slave of the state." A slave of the state. That, more or less, was how the court was to regard prisoners for the next hundred years, and its position meant that prisoners could be put to work on chain gangs, used as guinea pigs in painful or life-threatening scientific research, disciplined without a hearing, thrown into solitary for months at a stretch, forced to help pay prison costs by laboring in a prison industry, beaten and nearly starved, denied essential medical care, and much more. Prison authorities, the U.S. court system decreed, had the right to do just about as they pleased with those in their charge. A slave, after all, belongs to his or her master, and the law will not interfere between them on the slave's behalf. As the Supreme Court put it again in a 1962 decision, "supervision of inmates of . . . institutions rests with the proper administrative authorities and . . . courts have no power to supervise the management of disciplinary rules of such institutions."

Not only did prisoners have no legal rights, they had few human rights, either. Many prison officials and members of the public, in fact, seemed to forget that prisoners were individual human beings at all. It was the failure of authorities at New York's Attica State Prison to recognize the inmates as human like themselves that allowed them to limit each one to a single roll of toilet paper every five weeks. It allowed the same authorities to forbid prisoners to shower more than once a week, even in summertime when they were assigned to heavy outside labor. Not even children were seen as human once they entered a correctional institution. Before Jerome Miller took over as head of the Massachusetts juvenile system, some youngsters were being held under conditions that the public would find unacceptable in a public zoo.

By the time Miller did take over, though, things were changing, not only in Massachusetts but around the country. The prisoners' rights movement was underway.

In many ways, the movement was a direct outgrowth of the black civil rights movement of the 1950s and 1960s. Of course, prisoners were not alone in following the lead of the blacks in demanding their rights in those days. Hispanics, American Indians, the elderly and the handicapped, and many others were doing the same. But the prisoners' rights movement was linked to the civil rights effort with a special intensity, partly because civil rights leaders had often been arrested and jailed, so they were familiar with prison conditions, and partly because such a high percentage of U.S. prisoners are black.

By the early 1970s, prisoners were finding a variety of ways of making their voices heard outside their prison walls. At Attica and other institutions, they rioted. Violence is not an attractive way to make a point, but sometimes it can work. As a result of the Attica uprising, prisoners there won the right to two showers a week and—eventually—as much toilet paper as they needed.

In other instances, prisoners got in touch with prominent men and women in the outside world, begging them to use their influence to publicize their plight. *The New York Times* columnist Tom Wicker is one who became involved in prison reform efforts in this way. Jessica Mitford based much of the research for her muckraking book on prisons, *Kind and Usual Punishment: The Prison Business,* on mail she received from inmates in all parts of the country. Other citizens have become involved in prison reform efforts through being appointed by state governors to committees authorized to investigate riots and other prison problems. For many on such committees, this represented their first viewing of prisoners and prison conditions. The committees' recommendations nearly always included more sweeping and radical reforms than those of even the most progressive of corrections officials.

A third route by which prisoners' rights activists worked to improve their lot was through court challenges to certain prison practices. And now, almost for the first time, those challenges were bearing fruit. In 1971, a federal appeals court ruled in favor of a prisoner who had sued a warden for damages, claiming that he had been wrongfully confined in solitary for a year. The effect of that ruling was to establish that just because a person is a prisoner, he or she has not automatically lost all legal rights.

Since 1971, prisoners have continued to press the courts

for relief. Often they have gotten it. By 1985, twenty-nine separate correctional systems across the nation were under court order to improve their conditions of confinement. In addition, twenty-three had been ordered to reduce population levels. As we have seen, over half the states were under order to improve medical care for inmates. The courts have also decreed that prisoners must have access to law libraries and have compelled C.O.s and wardens to abandon systems of discipline enforced by prisoner-trusties. They have made it clear that prison authorities must meet certain minimum standards in their treatment of inmates—or face the closing down of their institutions.

Besides offering court challenges and using the publicity generated by riots and concerned individuals, the prisoners' rights movement has gotten an assist from organizations both public and private. Much help has come from the American Civil Liberties Union. It was through the ACLU that Jessica Mitford first became involved in writing about prisons. The ACLU's National Prison Project is an effort aimed at improving prison conditions and promoting the concept of community corrections. Church groups have also interested themselves in prisoner issues. The National Moratorium on Prison Construction, for instance, was formerly associated with the Unitarian-Universalist Service Committee; the Prison Research Education Action Project, headquartered in Orwell, Vermont, was set up by the New York State Council of Churches; and a Roman Catholic organization, the Christophers, dedicates itself in part to prison issues. Individual chaplains representing America's major faiths are among the most tireless workers in the nation's prisons. Other organizations directing their attention to prison reform, prisoner welfare, and prison alternatives include Volunteers of the Salvation Army, the National Council on Crime & Delinquency,

Aid to Incarcerated Mothers, The National Center for the Citizen Participation in the Administration of Justice and the National Coalition for Jail Reform. Activist prisoners and ex-prisoners have organized themselves, too. The California-based Prisoners' Union is one of the most important of inmate groups.

Even government agencies may help promote some of the goals of the prisoners' rights movement. The National Institute of Corrections, established by the Federal Bureau of Prisons in 1972, offers educational programs and training for prison professionals. One purpose of the Federal Correctional Institute (FCI), opened in North Carolina in 1976, is to test the usefulness of prison programs run by volunteers from outside.

Despite the efforts at reform, however, the prisoners' rights movement still has a long way to go. Although it can claim progress in the area of the legal standing of prisoners, it has accomplished little to erase the spirit of revenge and vindictiveness that has been part of U.S. prison systems almost from the start. According to Gene Stephens, professor at the College of Criminal Justice of the University of South Carolina in Columbia, such feelings actually grew during the middle and late 1970s. Stephens attributes this growth largely to the hard economic times that struck the nation during that period. "The economy fell," he wrote in a 1987 issue of *The Futurist* magazine. "Wages were frozen. Unemployment soared." As a result, Americans, worried about their own economic well-being, felt more resentment than usual toward those among them convicted of robbing, mugging, murdering, and raping—of, in other words, seeming determined to benefit themselves at the expense of the honest and law-abiding.

"By the end of the decade," Stephens wrote, "scores of scholars and practitioners wrote how 'nothing works' in rehabilitation, and the 'new realists' in criminology emerged

144

with a 'get tough' policy on crime. The criminal was . . . a pathological predator who should be eliminated. Forgiveness and rehabilitation were replaced by vindictiveness and retribution . . . . the lawbreaker who was no real threat in 'good times' became a true threat in the quest for scarce resources and a scapegoat for all that seemed to be wrong and unfair about society."

Does that suggest that Americans are about to turn the clock back and insist upon a return to the retributive punishments of yesteryear? Will tentative gropings in the direction of community corrections falter and the ideas of Graeme Newman and others like him win out after all? Not necessarily. As Stephens makes clear, the return of good economic times is likely to lead to yet another change in our attitude toward the incarcerated. What is more, the prisoners' rights movement and prisoner court challenges continue to make themselves felt.

Both are now getting a boost from a new source, the American Correctional Association. Under the leadership of Anthony P. Travisano, who took over as executive director of the ACA in 1974, that group has inaugurated a drive to improve prison conditions and make them more humane. The ACA also works to upgrade professionalism among prison staff members. To achieve its goals, the ACA has published a list of over six hundred standards for the nation's correctional institutions. The standards cover every aspect of prison life from food to living space, from schooling to recreation, and from working conditions to medical care and discipline. They are extremely specific, written in terms that penologists describe as "operational" and "measurable." C.O.s and wardens can be in no doubt as to their exact meaning. Cell space is to amount to sixty square feet per inmate. That's a standard that can be measured and verified. Prisoners are to get at least an hour of exercise daily. This, too, can be defined by num-

145

bers. Inmates accused of disciplinary violations must be offered legal representation at their hearings. That's an operational standard.

The new ACA standards are intended to guarantee that prison authorities will safeguard the legal and human rights of every single prisoner entrusted to them. They are aimed at providing inmates with decent treatment in the least restrictive environment possible. If the environment is that of a prerelease center, a group home, or some other community corrections setting, well and good. But even to the 10 or 20 percent of prisoners thought unfit for release, decent treatment must be offered. That, at least, is the stated aim of the ACA.

"We are shifting emphasis from the goal of reform or rehabilitation in prison," says Mary Ann Hawkes, a professor of sociology and criminal justice at Rhode Island College and an outspoken advocate of the ACA standards. "The emphasis today is on humane treatment." The whole idea that prisoners can be or even ought to be rehabilitated is questionable anyway, Dr. Hawkes contends. To rehabilitate means to restore to a former capacity, but what *decent* capacity have thieves, murderers, and sex offenders got to be restored *to*? The most a prison can do, Hawkes believes, is provide an atmosphere in which inmates can, if they wish, try to learn to function in a law-abiding society. Any prison that accomplishes this, she maintains, is doing its job. A prison's success can be measured only in terms of how humanely its inmates are treated and how much opportunity they have to take control of their own lives in a positive manner.

By that criterion, there are few successful prisons in the United States. Prisons that meet the bulk of the ACA standards for humane treatment can receive accreditation from that organization. Accreditation is an honor only; it conveys no legal standing. As of 1985, just sixteen states and the Federal Bureau of Prisons could claim one or more accredited prisons. The figures are worse than they sound, because of all the institutions so accredited, thirty were in the federal system, and another twenty-five in Florida, twelve in Illinois, and ten in Oklahoma. Those seventy-seven facilities accounted for 58 percent—over half—of all the prisons that met ACA standards.

What of the future? Will the prisons of the twenty-first century move to treat inmates more humanely, spurred on by the desire for ACA approval, or under the impetus of court order? Will the NIC and other organizations manage to raise the level of professionalism among prison staffers? Will groups like NMPC and NCIA succeed in making community corrections a reality for the majority of convicted criminals? Will American voters begin informing themselves about the harsh realities of prison life—and seek to change them once and for all?

Or will our prison systems continue down the path they have followed over the last two centuries? That path has led, over and over, from brutal treatment and a spirit of vengefulness to unrest and rioting, then to efforts at reform and finally, to new cruelties and brutalities. It is a path that has, for two hundred years, kept Americans building, staffing and maintaining prisons equipped to do little more than reinforce the negative attitudes and behaviors that filled their cells in the first place.

What way for our prisons? The answer depends upon so many factors: on the crime rate, on the courts, on what politicians think and say, on what happens behind bars over the next months and years. But most of all, it depends upon us, the American people. It is we the people who have made our prisons and their problems what they are today. It is we who will determine the nature of prisons—or their alternatives—in the next century.

147

Glossary

appeal—The request by either side in a criminal case that a higher court review the ruling of a lower court.

bail—A sum of money posted by a criminal defendant. Once the money has been put up, the defendant remains free until the trial. If the defendant does not appear for trial, the bail money is forfeited.

capital punishment—The death penalty.

Comprehensive Crime Control Act of 1984—Federal crime law passed by the U.S. Congress. It provides, among other things, for uniform sentencing in federal cases through the use of sentencing guidelines promulgated by a commission on sentencing and attempts to deal more firmly than before with white-collar crime.

corporal punishment—The inflicting of physical pain.

felony—A serious crime, such as theft, murder, or rape. A felony is punishable by a prison sentence. The person who commits a felony is called a felon.

Intensive Supervision Program—Probation or parole with extra-strict conditions, such as daily meetings with a parole officer. Amounts to a form of house arrest.

jail—Facility for detaining persons pending trial on the charges upon which they face. Convicted criminals are not usually housed in jails. On the federal level, jails are known as Detention Centers. On the state level, they have varying names, such as Awaiting Trial Unit or Intake Service Center.

misdemeanor—A crime that is considered less serious than a felony. Anyone who commits a misdemeanor is called a misdemeanant, and can be sentenced to less than one year in a jail.

parole—System whereby prisoners are released, usually because they have displayed good behavior in prison, before having completed their sentences.

penitentiary—Type of prison that dates back to reforms introduced by Quakers in the late eighteenth century. Penitentiary prisoners were supposed to be induced to repent sincerely of their crimes.

penology—The study of prison management and the treatment of offenders.

plea bargain—To admit guilt for a lesser offence than the one first brought. Successful plea bargaining results in a lesser sentence.

pre-release center—Facility for prisoners who are just about to be freed. Inmates of a pre-release center may have jobs in the outside world, extensive visiting hours, and other privileges not allowed in prison.

preventive detention—Practice, approved by the U.S. Supreme Court in 1987, which permits judges to refuse bail to any defendant considered to be a danger to the community or to a particular individual.

prison—Institution for incarceration of criminals convicted of felonies.

probation—System whereby a convicted person's prison sentence is suspended. Probationers must check in regularly with an officer of the court, and violations of the conditions of probation may result in the original prison sentence being carried out.

prosecutor—Lawyer who presents the government's case against a defendant.

reformatory—Type of prison for youth and young adult criminals pioneered in the United States in the late 1800s. Its aim was to remake the characters of its inmates.

recidivism—A falling back into criminal ways.

restitution—Repayment by a criminal to his or her victim or to a fund for general victim compensation. It may take the form of money, volunteer labor, or some type of service to the community as a whole.

uniform sentencing—The use of sentencing guidelines to promote criminal penalties that are consistent from court to court and judge to judge. A major provision of the Comprehensive Crime Control Act of 1984, uniform sentencing is intended to overcome past unfairnesses in the handing out of prison terms.

Further Reading

BOOKS

Alper, Benedict S. *Prisons Inside-out: Alternatives in Correctional Reform,* Cambridge: Ballinger Publishing Company, 1974.

Bender, David L. and Bruno Leone, Series Eds., Bonnie Szumski, book ed. *America's Prisons: Opposing Viewpoints.* St. Paul: Greenhaven Press, 1985.

Blom-Cooper, Louis, ed. *Progress in Penal Reform,* Oxford: Clarendon Press, 1974.

Camp, George M. and Camille Graham Camp. *The Corrections Yearbook,* South Salem: Criminal Justice Institute, Inc., 1985.

Clark, Phyllis Elperin and Robert Lehrman. *Doing Time: A Look at Crime and Prisons,* New York: Hastings House, Publishers, 1980.

Harris, Janet. *Crisis in Corrections: The Prison Problem,* New York: McGraw-Hill Book Company, 1973.

Harris, Jean. *Stranger in Two Worlds,* New York: Macmillan, 1986. International Directory of Correctional Administrations, College Park, MD: American Correctional Association, 1987.

LeShan, Eda. *The Roots of Crime: What You Need to Know About Crime and What You Can Do About It,* New York: Four Winds Press, 1981.

Mitford, Jessica. *Kind & Usual Punishment: The Prison Business,* New York: Random House Inc., 1974.

PERIODICALS

Applebome, Peter. "New Prisoners Are Barred By Crowded Texas Prisons." *The New York Times,* January 17, 1987.

—"1,000 New Inmates a Week Jam Too Few Cells." *The New York Times,* March 1, 1987.

Armstrong, Scott. "East Los Angeles says 'no' to proposed state prison." *The Christian Science Monitor,* September 22, 1986.

Beebe, Jeff. "No such thing as an empty bed." *Kennebec Journal,* March 29, 1986.

Brozan, Nadine. "Prisoners Learn How to Be Good Fathers." *The New York Times,* September 29, 1986.

Bruske, Ed. "A Law Meets Reality—And Loses." *The Washington Post,* May 11, 1986.

—"Drug Treatment Shortage Keeps Addicts in Jail." *The Washington Post,* May 14, 1986.

Campbell, Catherine. "The Politics of Prison Industries." *The California Prisoner,* November 1986.

Clendinen, Dudley. "Dilemma for Southern Prosecutors: Infect Streets or Prison with AIDS?" *The New York Times,* January 2, 1987.

Corwin, Miles. "Prison is a state of mind at minimum-security lockup." *Daily Record,* August 31, 1986.

Cox, Meg. "Theater Group Plays to Captive Audience—In Prison System." *The Wall Street Journal,* October 17, 1986.

"Crime Rate Is Put at a 13-Year Low." *The New York Times,* October 9, 1986.

"Delaware Prisoners Finding Careers at 50¢ a Day." *The New York Times,* March 1, 1987.

Glover, Alexandra H. "Prisons are jammed, but few people want new ones as neighbors." *The Christian Science Monitor,* July 21, 1986.

Greenberg, Joel. "Bruce Danto and the Crime of Jail Suicide." *Science News,* Vol. 129, June 14, 1986.

Henderson, Keith. "Halfway house that's all in the family." *The Christian Science Monitor,* October 14, 1986.

—"Southern states innovate to save jail space." *The Christian Science Monitor,* March 21, 1986.

"Inmates in Solitary Sue Massachusetts on Rights." *The New York Times,* February 8, 1987.

Kreis, Donald M. "In the dark corners of the Maine correctional system, some inmates live like 'mushrooms.' Overcrowding is just part of the problem." *The Maine Times,* May 9, 1986.
—"Prison Reform." *The Maine Times,* May 16, 1986.
Kurtz, Howard. "Rules for Uniform Sentencing, End to Early Parole Proposed." *The Washington Post,* September 30, 1986.
McBride, Nicholas C. "Proposed guidelines ending federal parole are widely criticized." *The Christian Science Monitor,* April 8, 1987.
McDonald, Maureen. "Sentencing rules would rate crimes." *USA Today,* April 14, 1987.
"Maryland Town Embraces Prison It Opposed." *The New York Times,* December 21, 1986.
May, Clifford D. "Electronic 'Ankle of the Law' Jails L.I. Man." *The New York Times,* December 9, 1986.
Noble, Kenneth B. "U.S. Sentencing Plan Urges Fixed Terms and No Parole." *The New York Times,* April 12, 1987.
"Official blames riot on 'hard-core' inmates." *Kennebec Journal,* April 3, 1986.
Pear, Robert. "What Alien Law Will Mean: Some Questions and Answers." *The New York Times,* October 26, 1986.
Peterson, Iver. "How to Stay Out on Bail When You're Out of Cash? Charge It!" *The New York Times,* November 27, 1986.
Press, Aric. "Inside America's Toughest Prison." *Newsweek,* October 6, 1986.
"Private firms ready to take over nation's prisons." *Daily Record,* December 2, 1986.
Purnick, Joyce: "City Plans to Add 2,300 Jail Spaces." *The New York Times,* October 9, 1986.
Remal, Gary. "'Prison without walls being readied." *Kennebec Journal,* September 2, 1986.
Sitomer, Curtis J. "Courts move to break the shackles of forced drugging." *The Christian Science Monitor,* June 26, 1986.
Smerling, Terry. "New Jails Won't End Overcrowding." *Los Angeles Times,* September 5, 1986.
Stephens, Gene. "Crime and Punishment." *The Futurist,* January-February, 1987.

Steptoe, Sonja. "Inmates Claim Prisons Are Failing to Provide Adequate Medical Care." *The Wall Street Journal,* May 15, 1986.

Taylor, Stuart Jr. "Bail Denial: Open Debate." *The New York Times,* May 28, 1987.

Tharp, Mike. 'Oregon's Overcrowded Prisons Reflect a Nationwide Problem." *The Wall Street Journal,* April 28, 1987.

Timnick, Lois. "Jail Suicides: Do They Represent a Flaw in the System?" *Los Angeles Times,* October 23, 1986.

Toby, Jackson. "Worst Thing About U.S. Prisons Is the Prisoners." *The Wall Street Journal,* June 10, 1986.

Tolchin, Martin. "As Privately Owned Prisons Increase, So Do Their Critics." *The New York Times,* February 11, 1985.

—"Jails Run by Private Company Force It to Face Question of Accountability." *The New York Times,* February 19, 1985.

Werner, Leslie Maitland. "Getting Out the Word On the New Crime Act." *The New York Times,* November 16, 1984.

Wilkerson, Isabel. "Indiana Case Kindles a Debate on Death Sentence for Juveniles." *The New York Times,* October 28, 1986.

Wolfgang, Marvin E., "A Return to 'Just Deserts.'" *The Key Reporter,* Vol. 52, No. 1, Autumn 1986.

Addresses

Aid to Incarcerated Mothers
St. Paul's Cathedral
138 Tremont St., 4th Fl.
Boston, MA 02111

American Correctional
    Association
4321 Hartwick Rd.
Suite L208
College Park, MD 20740

Federal Bureau of Prisons
320 First St. NW
Washington, D.C. 20534

Federal Correctional Institute
Old North Carolina Highway,
    #75
Butner, NC 27509

National Center on Institutions
    and Alternatives
814 St. Asaph St.
Alexandria, VA 22314

National Coalition for Jail
    Reform
1828 L St. NW
Suite 1200
Washington, D.C. 20036

National Council on Crime &
    Delinquency
77 Maiden La., 4th Fl.
San Francisco, CA 94108

National Institute of Corrections
320 First St. NW, Rm. 207
Washington, D.C. 20534

National Moratorium on Prison
    Construction
309 Pennsylvania Av. SW
Washington, D.C. 20003

National Prison Project
1346 Connecticut Av. NW, Suite
    402
Washington, D.C. 20036

Prisoners' Union
1317 Eighteenth St.
San Francisco, CA 94107

Prison Research Education
    Action Project
Shoreham Depot Rd.
Orwell, VT 05760

The Christophers
12 E. 48th St.
New York, NY 10017

The National Center for Citizen
    Participation in the
    Administration of Justice
20 West St., 4th Fl.
Boston, MA 02111

Volunteers of America
3813 N. Causeway Blvd.
Metairie, LA 70002

Index

minimum-security prisons, 38, 56, 99
Missouri State Penitentiary, 12, 101
Mitford, Jessica, 142-143
Mockler, Rick, 12-13

N

National Center for the Citizen Participation in the Administration of Justice, 144
National Center on Institutions and Alternatives, 126, 128-129, 135, 147
National Coalition for Jail Reform, 144
National Commission for the Protection of Human Subjects of Biomedical and Behavioral Research, 104
National Council on Crime and Delinquency, 143
National Institute of Corrections, 144
National Moratorium on Prison Construction (NMPC), 126, 128-129, 135, 143, 147
National Prison Project, 143
Newman, Graeme R., 102-106, 145
New York State Council of Churches, 143
Nissen, Ted, 116-119
Nixon, President Richard M., 52

O

Oglethorp, James, 19
overcrowding, in prisons, 10, 97-101, 113-114, 120, 126

P

parole, 29, 47-48, 65-66, 98, 113
Patuxent Institution, 31, 103
Pennsylvania State Correctional Institution, 91

Penitentiary Act of 1779, 25
prerelease centers, 39, 47, 87, 136
Prison Congress, 28, 53
Prison Research Education Action Project (PREAP), 49, 58, 143
prisoners' rights movement, 13, 141-144, 146
Prisoners' Union, 13, 144
private prisons, 116-119, 121
Prohibition, 36-37, 51
probation, 47-48, 131-132
psychological counseling, 31, 39, 103, 106, 119
punishment, in history, 17-31

Q

Quakers, 25-26, 32, 40, 102-103, 139

R

racial problems in prisons, 91-92
recidivism, 98-101, 105, 114, 119-120, 127
reform schools, 28-30, 41
Ricci, Kenneth, 98, 114
Rideau, Wilbert, 15-17, 32-33, 68
Riker's Island, 46-47, 91, 106
riots, in prisons, 9-11, 107
Rutgers University Institute for Criminological Research, 11

S

Sargent, Francis, 124, 136
sentencing, 64-65, 68-69
  fixed, 28-29, 66-67
  indeterminate, 29-30, 41
  innovative, 134-135
  mandatory, 113
  uniform, 64-66
silent system, 27-28, 30, 40

159

Silva, Sergeant Gerald, 128
Sinclair, Billy, 68
Smerling, Judge Terry, 137
Snellings, Travis, 116-117, 119
social workers, 31, 39, 72, 106
solitary confinement, 26-28, 30-31, 40, 74
State of the Prisons in England and Wales, The, 24-25
state prison systems, 40-44, 46
State University of New York at Albany, 102
Stephens, Gene, 144
street crime, 54-55, 57-58, 67

T

Texas Department of Corrections, 101, 113
Thornton, Charles, 57
Tilton, Peter J., 131
Toby, Jackson, 11-12, 92
Travisano, Anthony P., 145

U

Unheavenly City, The, 52
Unitarian-Universalist Service Committee, 143
U.S. Congress, 35, 37, 63, 67
U.S. Constitution, 25-26, 32, 134
U.S. Department of Defense, 56
U.S. Department of Justice, 37, 55, 65, 97, 109
U.S. Public Health Service, 119
U.S. Sentencing Commission, 64
U.S. Supreme Court, 15-16, 33, 45, 60, 68, 140-141

V

Vilain, Jean Jacques, 24
violence, in prisons, 11, 98, 100-101, 109, 114, 120, 126

vocational programs, 85, 99-100, 106-107, 114
Volunteers of the Salvation Army, 143

W

West Virginia Penitentiary, 91
white-collar crime, 55-60, 63, 67, 130
Wicker, Tom, 142
women's prisons, 71-82, 91
work-release systems, 127-128